9.29

THE BILLION-DOLLAR CONNECTION

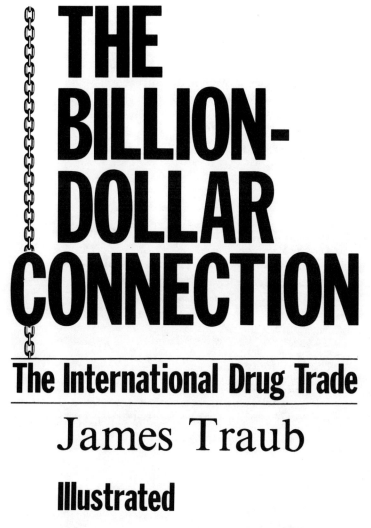

THE BILLION-DOLLAR CONNECTION

The International Drug Trade

James Traub

Illustrated

Julian Messner
New York

Manufactured in the United States of America

Design by Irving Perkins Associates
Maps by Mary Leto
Library of Congress Cataloging in Publication Data.

Library of Congress Cataloging in Publication Data

Traub, James.
  The billion-dollar connection.

  Bibliography: p.
  Includes index.
  1. Narcotics. 2. Narcotics, Control of.
3. Drug abuse—United States. I. Title.
HV5801.T72   1982   363.4'5   82-14212
ISBN 0-671-45247-9

CONTENTS

INTRODUCTION

On the Lower East Side of New York a peddler is walking up and down the sidewalk, crying, "Red tape! Green tape! Best you can find." Around him people are selling shirts and socks and leather goods, but this man is a heroin dealer advertising his products, in broad daylight. A bag of heroin sealed with a green tape, for example, comes from Iran. If you want to buy, you are taken to a booth where your "tracks"—your needle marks— are examined, to make sure that you're an addict, not a cop. If you pass the test you push some money, maybe $20, through a hole in a door and get back from underneath the door a little plastic package on a sheet of cardboard—a single hit.

In Los Angeles an executive with a record company or an advertising firm, or an actor or singer, meets in a fancy ranch house with his elegantly dressed cocaine dealer. The customer admires the pure white crystals, presented to him in a snuffbox or fine tobacco pouch, and dabs a bit on his tongue or sniffs some through a nostril to test its purity. He smiles and peels off perhaps twenty $100 bills for a single ounce.

At a high school baseball game a student wanders in and out of the crowd, looking as if he's minding his own business. But as he walks around he says, under his breath, "Loose joints, loose joints." By the third inning he's already sold two dozen joints, and he leaves, $25 richer.

These are scenes that most everyone has seen or heard about—scenes from the drug business. Drugs are a business like fast food or cars or movies, with the difference, first, that drugs are illegal, and second, that they are hazardous to your health. Because drugs are illegal and because people are often desperate to get them, selling drugs is just about the world's most profitable business. Think of someone paying $2,000 for an ounce of something.

People in the drug business are in it for one thing only—money. Maybe the student who sells joints at a ball game makes only enough to buy a used car, but the people on top, the people who live in South America and Hong Kong and Italy and Miami and New York, live in palatial homes and drive Rolls-Royces and throw away a million dollars gambling as if it were lunch money. Some of them don't even use drugs themselves; they go into whatever crime pays the most—prostitution, gambling, drugs. Those who get in the way—rival criminals, government officials, the police—are bribed or threatened or killed. This is the part of the drug business that nobody sees, except when a war between two drug gangs makes the headlines or when the police come up with a big bust.

The invisible world of the drug business is the subject of this book. The deal in which the drug user pays the pusher is only the last in a long series of deals that stretch across borders and over oceans and into foreign cities and beyond to the impoverished villages where drugs are grown in the first place. And the moment when the police arrest a dealer is only the last in a long series of confrontations between the people who make a living off drugs and the people who enforce drug laws. The story of the drug business is a tale of secret caravans through the jungle, trucks with hidden panels and compartments racing down lonely roads at night, sophisticated laboratories in which drugs are "cooked" from raw sap or paste, "runners" and "couriers" trying to slip past customs officials at airports and border crossings, stolen planes and boats and guns, ruthless murder and corruption, swift and efficient networks of people who break down drugs into ever smaller quantities until they can be sold on the streets.

And at every step of the way the police cast a shadow. In foreign countries they burn fields of opium and cocaine and marijuana, and they try to intercept those caravans and trucks and planes. In the United States they try to break up the rings, including the Mafia-dominated ones, which control the distribution of drugs; they try to stop the drugs at the border or even at sea just beyond the border. Most of the time the drug business wins, because it has more money and, sometimes, more ingenuity. It is hard to imagine how rich and powerful drug operators are. In 1981 an estimated 60 billion dollars' worth of illegal drugs were sold in the United States. That is more money than all but the two or three biggest companies in the world take in, and more than most entire countries spend in a year. During that same time police and government officials spent about 500 million dollars on enforcing drug laws. So it's easy to see why the battle is uneven. Police efforts around the world decrease the amount available and make drugs more expensive, but they barely make a dent in the drug problem.

One thing which this book is *not* about is what drugs do to you if you use them. There are other books available on that subject. But the fact is that the killings and the bribes and the wild profits would not exist if drugs had not been made illegal all over the world; and they would not have been outlawed if they were not harmful. If narcotics were legal rival gangs would not murder one another in order to control their distribution, and middlemen would not jack up the price ten times over before passing the drugs along to the next stage. Heroin would be as cheap as many medicines; marijuana as many ordinary plants. But between the farmer and the user come the "mules," who carry it from the fields, the hideaways, the high-priced chemists, the vast army of smugglers carrying it across the border, the planes and boats, the long trips back and forth to baffle the police.

But the real reason for the high price of illegal narcotics is that the people who use them want them so much that they will pay practically any price. Even with all the evasions and the trickery which brings drugs to the street-corner, they could be sold far more cheaply than they are. But the price can be multiplied again and again, so that the cost to a heroin addict may be a thousand times the value to an opium farmer, or more, because the addict is desperate. A butcher can charge only so much for a pound of steak, since no matter how much his customers love steak, they can always eat something else if it gets too expensive. A pusher can charge incredible amounts of money for tiny bags of heroin, because, even though most of his customers are poor, they cannot live without his product. They'll find the money to pay for it somehow, usually by crime. As a world of crime stretches from the farmer to the user, so it stretches, at least in the case of the heroin addict, from the user to the society he victimizes. Marijuana and cocaine are not, of course, addictive, but they are powerfully habit-forming. Regular users come to depend on them so heavily that they are willing to pay their high price.

This feverish desire for drugs tells us a great deal about why they are illegal. At a certain point dependency becomes something like slavery, or at the very least, helplessness. The heroin user rapidly becomes a heroin addict. Some addicts are able to function, but many come to inhabit a separate world, divided between the trance of being "strung out," and the panic of hunting for money to supply the fix. And there is always the danger of the overdose, as the addiction grows more and more demanding. In 1980 over 600 people died from an overdose. Famous rock stars like Jimi Hendrix and Janis Joplin have been killed by heroin.

While less destructive physically, cocaine can also lead to dependence and helplessness. A number of sports figures have confessed that cocaine habits running into the hundreds of thousands of dollars a year have brought their careers close to ruins. Actor John Belushi completely destroyed his body, and eventually himself, through an enormous cocaine habit, combined with alcohol and heroin. And the use of cocaine is growing faster than that of any other drug. Between 1978 and 1979 the number of Americans who had used cocaine in the previous year jumped from 6.5 million to 9.7 million. The number of people admitted to hospital emergency rooms for cocaine-related injuries more than tripled between 1976 and 1981, while the number of cocaine-related deaths quadrupled in the same period. And although cocaine has a reputation as a "rich man's drug," the number of high school students who use it has increased dramatically.

It is easy to scoff at the idea that marijuana is dangerous, partially because its danger has been wildly exaggerated in the past. But nobody needs a medical report to know that frequent marijuana smokers do not function the way others do. They, too, surrender to the drug. People who smoke marijuana often lose their ability to think sharply and remember quickly, and lose their interest in practically everything except what happens to be right in front of them. And marijuana has been getting considerably stronger over the last ten years, as the more powerful Colombian variety has replaced the Mexican plant. This, combined with the fact that heavy users have become more common has made marijuana smoking a more serious medical problem. In 1976 10 percent of the patients in federal drug-treatment programs were there because of marijuana; by 1979 the figure had risen to 16 percent.

From the point of view of cost, or physical harm, marijuana, cocaine, and heroin can hardly be compared to each other. But the one thing that unites all of these drugs is that a great many dead bodies and corrupted politicians and threatened judges lie between the farmer who grows them and the user who smokes or snorts or injects them. Cigarettes may be bad for you, but nobody gets killed delivering them to the store. But cocaine, for example, definitely harms a great many people on its way to you: the farmers who are paid pitifully for their coca leaf; the police, as well as the entire economy of Colombia or Bolivia, who are corrupted by drug money; the citizens of southern Florida, where most cocaine enters the United States, who find themselves living in America's most violent area; and the innocent people who get caught in the cross fire of cocaine wars. The same is true, to a much greater extent, with heroin, though to a lesser degree, with marijuana. One way or another, drugs kill.

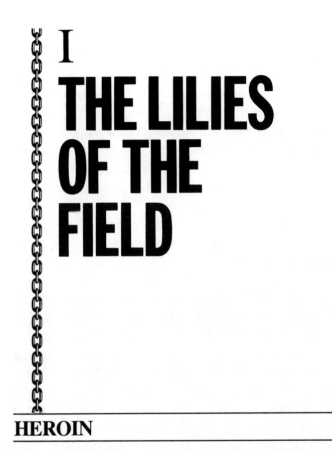

I
THE LILIES OF THE FIELD

HEROIN

HEROIN IS a finished product made, after several operations, from the sap of an opium poppy. It is grown by poor farmers, usually in tiny fields in hilly areas with fairly poor soil. As far as most of these farmers are concerned, opium is not a terrible drug but just one more crop, like corn or rice or beans. Opium simply pays better than the others: with a good crop perhaps they will be able to feed their hungry families a little bit better than usual. In many places opium is also grown as a medicine, since it dulls pain. Boiled down, and with the addition of

15

some chemicals, it can be turned into morphine, which doctors all over the world use to prevent people from feeling pain. In fact the word "heroin" was invented by the Bayer Company, the people who make the aspirin, who found, in the early part of this century, that a combination of morphine and a chemical called acetic anhydride could be used as a very powerful cough medicine. What they didn't see was that the same combination could be an addictive drug.

During the nineteenth century people used opium fairly casually, though it was frowned upon by many. The famous fictional detective Sherlock Holmes sometimes smoked opium to help him solve problems. The great English poet Samuel Taylor Coleridge claimed that he wrote several of his poems after smoking opium. The English even made vast quantities of opium available to the Chinese to keep them quiet and obedient during the time when much of China was an English colony. But with the invention of heroin, addiction became a problem in Europe and the United States. By 1924 the sale of heroin had become illegal in the United States, but it was too late: organized crime had seen an opportunity for a profit, and soon the forerunners of today's Mafia were buying opium in the Middle East, especially Turkey, and turning it into heroin in laboratories in China as well as southern France. One of the most notorious mobsters of the century, Lucky Luciano, organized the modern Mafia in the 1930s with heroin as a key business—in part to keep prostitutes addicted and thus make them dependent on the gangsters who profited from them.

For forty years, as the number of addicts grew, Turkey

remained the world's most important source of heroin. Finally, in the early 1970s, as the addict population of the United States grew beyond half a million, the supply of Turkish heroin was destroyed in a case that became famous as "the French connection." It was called the French connection because what was destroyed was not the opium crop but the laboratories in Marseille, a port city in southern France, where opium was made into heroin and then shipped to the United States. At the same time, in 1973, the Turkish government banned the growing of opium, though later it decided that a small amount could be grown for use as morphine.

By the early 1970s narcotics officials thought that the terrible heroin problem had been beaten. But just as Turkey was closing down, two new areas were opening up: Mexico and Southeast Asia. By now there was so much money in heroin that organized crime groups and others were determined to go into it no matter what the police did. They sought out countries with weak or corrupt governments, and worked with tribes or clans who were hostile to the government; when one area was shut down, they moved to another. In the mid-1970s another major police effort cut off the supply of Mexican heroin, and once again it seemed that the heroin menace had been turned back. And then heroin began appearing from yet another corner of the globe: Southwest Asia, primarily Pakistan. And a few years after Mexican heroin was crushed it began to reappear. In 1981 America's half-million or so addicts were supplied with roughly four tons of heroin from Mexico, Pakistan, and Southeast Asia, mostly Burma. In order to understand why people grow opium and how it is made into heroin, as well as how it is smuggled out of the country where it is produced, we will look briefly at Pakistan, and then take a longer look at Southeast Asia.

PAKISTAN

Farmers have been growing opium in Iran, Afghanistan, and Pakistan for centuries. Opium smoking has long been popular in this area, especially in Iran, which has between 500,000 and 2 million opium addicts, out of a total of 35 million people. As a result, the opium grown here has traditionally remained inside these three countries. Now, however, American drug enforcement officials feel more worried about heroin from Pakistan than from any other area. In 1980 Pakistan alone grew 600 tons of opium, which can be made into 60 tons of heroin—far more than the world can use. Most of the opium is planted along the border between Pakistan and Afghanistan, an area called the North-West Frontier Province (NWFP). No government controls this area; it is run by a fierce tribe known as the Pathans, who act as if they were a nation all by themselves. Many of the Pathans live in a mountainous area that can be reached only on foot; even the less wild regions have only a single road running through them, and that is often passable only by jeep. In addition, practically every male Pathan carries a gun, even if it's the kind used by the American army during World War I. If the Pathans want to grow opium, they grow opium.

In Pakistan as elsewhere, opium is planted in the fall,

Opium pod and blossom. When the blossom withers, the opium is ready for harvest. (DRUG ENFORCEMENT ADMINISTRATION)

after the rainy season. By spring the mountain slopes are waving with the slender stalks of the poppy, each topped with a round pod, and then by blossoms. When the pod has become full and the blossoms wither, the farmer makes two or three horizontal cuts in its side. Within a day the milky sap that was inside the pod has oozed out and dried, and the farmer scrapes it off with a dull knife. By the time he has finished his harvest, the farmer has a dense square of opium gum.

Most farmers in this mountainous region have tiny plots of land, usually two or three acres. Of these, the farmer may devote one acre to poppies, producing about 15 pounds of opium. In a good year a farmer could receive $1,000 or more for his crop. By American

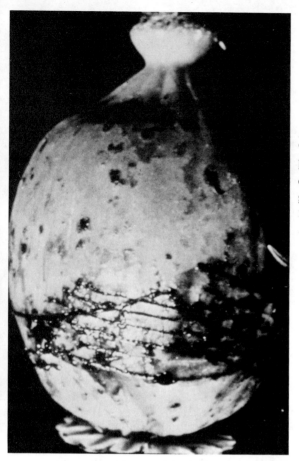

An incised opium pod. The farmer makes horizontal slashes in order to let the opium gum ooze out. (DRUG ENFORCEMENT ADMINISTRATION)

Opium poppies in the Golden Crescent—ready to harvest. (DRUG ENFORCEMENT ADMINISTRATION)

standards this sounds like next to nothing, but the average Pakistani farmer earns only $200 a year. It should come as no surprise that practically every farmer in the region grows opium and talks about the crop in the same tones that a Virginia farmer uses in discussing tobacco. Of course, if you grow too much of something, the price goes down, and in the late 1970s the price of opium suddenly dropped from $200 a kilogram (2.2 pounds) to $50 a kilo. So farmers started growing a bit less.

At the end of the season the opium is taken down the hills, and much of it lands in a town called Landi Kotal. Landi Kotal is one of the smuggling capitals of the world. Black marketeers sell refrigerators, color television sets, trucks, guns of any and all descriptions, and, of course, opium. The opium is sold openly. One reporter who went into the area walked into a shop to buy some chocolate and was asked if he wouldn't prefer 20 kilos of pure heroin, worth perhaps $40 million on the streets of New York. Even his rickshaw driver offered him heroin—this in an area that until recently didn't even have the laboratories to produce heroin from opium. Opium also sits in huge stacks behind shops, waiting for buyers.

Once opium is bought, arrangements can be made to have it smuggled. Sometimes the opium has already been converted to what is called morphine base, a refined version that weighs only one-tenth as much. The opium or morphine base may then be taken to Karachi, a major city on the Arabian Sea, where it is secretly carried on to a plane bound for Europe or the United States, or it may be loaded on to mules or into the trunks of cars for a long journey across the wild spaces of Central Asia. Here another independent tribe, the Kurds, takes over. The

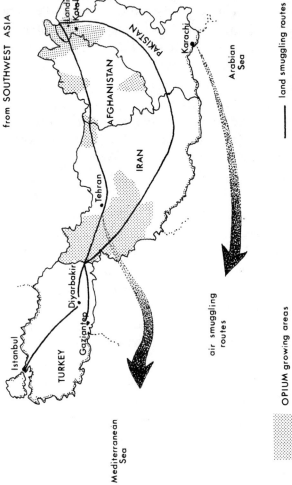

Kurds, like the Pathans, respect ancient, unofficial tribal boundaries, not national borders. At home in no one nation, the Kurds range across the northern portions of Pakistan, Afghanistan, Iran, Iraq, and Turkey. For centuries they have led caravans across this vast region; now the caravans, sometimes by car and sometimes by mule, transport opium instead of silk.

As recently as 1976 virtually no heroin at all reached the United States from Southwest Asia. Only three years later 40 percent of American heroin was coming from that area. When one source of heroin is wiped out, another pops up. And this can happen quickly because opium is almost always grown in parts of the world where the government has little power. Opium is illegal in Pakistan, and the current government of President Zia ul-Haq has seriously tried to enforce the laws. But in large parts of northwestern Pakistan, the government owns only the main road, while the tribes control the rest. The last thing the government wants to do is provoke this warlike tribe. And on the other side of the border, in Afghanistan, a war is raging with the Russians, and the situation is even further out of control. What is bad for a country—civil war and turmoil, the hostility of native groups—is ideal for the production and smuggling of drugs. And the world will probably never lack for remote, hilly areas beyond the reach of governments, or for poor farmers in need of extra income.

SOUTHEAST ASIA

Americans have a hard time understanding why farmers halfway across the world are willing to grow crops that ultimately lead to so much anguish and death. Why don't they stop, and grow something else? Perhaps if we try to see the problem from the point of view of the farmer in the notorious Golden Triangle—the mountainous jungle where Thailand, Burma, and Laos meet—we will be less surprised.

The innumerable tribes or ethnic groups of the Golden Triangle—the Wah, the Aka, the Karen, the Hmong— have lived the same simple life for centuries. The combination of mountain and jungle means that many live in areas with no roads at all, a day's walk from the nearest market, weeks away from even a small city. Their homes are mud huts, and their meals consist of little besides rice. What little they grow, they eat themselves, and few have much surplus to send into town to trade for goods. In a bad year they may not have enough rice even for themselves. Without opium, hunger is always a possibility; with it, they will still be poor, but at least they will have some money as insurance. The average Thai farmer, like the Pathan, earns about $200 a year; for a single kilo of opium he may receive over $100.

The Thai or Burmese farmer has no knowledge of the connection between opium and the tragedy of heroin addiction. Cut off from the outside world, he knows opium only as the substance that his tribe has been growing and smoking since as far back as memory and legend go. Among the hill tribes it is considered normal for old men to smoke opium, especially in the evening; it is normal, in fact, throughout Southeast Asia. Opium is far less powerful and dangerous than heroin, and as long as smoking is confined to the aged, it does no harm to the working life of the village.

The headman of a Hmong village neatly summed up the situation to author Frank Robertson:

> The government asked us to stop growing opium. We are loyal to the King, because he brings things that we need, and when we are sick he sends a doctor to take care of us. So now we are growing beans, peppers, carrots and apricots because that is what the King wants us to do. But we cannot make enough money from those. When the merchants buy our opium, they come here and pay 2,000 baht [$150] per kilogram. We get extra money because they pay our people to carry it to town. The vegetables and the fruit we have to take to town ourselves, more than a day's walk. The town merchants are bad men. They offer us a bad price because they know that these things spoil. Opium does not rot, so if we think the price is too low, we just keep it. We don't know what happens to the opium when it leaves here. Government people have told us that it is made into heroin, and that is a very bad thing. We don't know anything about that. We only smoke opium. After a hard day's work it is good to relax, and it keeps us healthy.

Thailand's king, as the villager said, has started a program, with American officials from the Agency for International Development, to substitute food crops for opium. Programs of this sort exist almost everywhere that drugs are grown, and the Thai program is not much more successful than are most others. The Thai government has hired local farmers to destroy opium crops; at the same time, though, it fears angering the hill people, who might join forces with rebels. Even the handful of villages now proclaimed opium-free are, in most cases, still growing some opium. Another problem is illustrated by a United Nations development program in the hill area. The wells that have been sunk with U.N. money have been used mostly to provide an irrigation system for opium, instead of the new crops that the U.N. group has provided.

Everywhere in the world drugs are braided together with politics, but nowhere more tightly than in Southeast Asia. Two events have made the Golden Triangle into one one of the world's leading narcotics producers: the Chinese Revolution, in 1948, and the Vietnam War. When the communists took over in China, troops loyal to the deposed leader, Chiang Kai-shek, fled in several directions. One group, known as the Fifth Kuomingtang Army (KMT) headed south across the border to Burma. The KMT Army was determined to carry on the war from there, but they were running short of guns and material. In need of money, they discovered what every succeeding rebel group in Southeast Asia had found: the best source of currency is opium. And they discovered something else that also held true later on: the American CIA was willing to look the other way in the interest of helping "friends." It would even actively assist in developing the opium trade. The CIA, according to Frank Robertson, author of *Triangle of Death*, was supplying the KMT with money and material as it organized the opium business in Burma and Thailand, though it rapidly became clear that the army was not about to undo the revolution, and the Burmese did not need their defense against China.

Until the KMT Army came along, opium used to find its way from the secluded villages to the large cities of

Asia in small batches, by various routes. The KMT Army organized a system, sending its own buying agents into the villages, sending vast caravans winding through Burma and Thailand to the lowlands, paying off policemen and government officials to ensure that the opium safely reached the coast. Eventually the KMT Army forgot about its political aims and became little more than a trafficking group. And it set a pattern: as the politics of Southeast Asia became more chaotic, more groups sprang up to challenge governments, turning to opium for money and finally becoming very little different from bands of smugglers. The difference, in Southeast Asia, is that the drug trade is controlled by entire armies with thousands of troops and modern weapons.

Until the arrival of American soldiers in the area, though, the amount of money to be made in the drug trade was limited by the number of opium smokers in Bangkok, Hong Kong, Singapore, and the other great cities of the region. This is no small number: 100,000 of Hong Kong's 4 million people and 85 percent of its prisoners are addicted to opium or heroin. But Americans, even American soldiers, arrived with unheard-of amounts of money. As anger and disgust among the troops mounted, so did heroin use. By the middle of 1971, between 25,000 and 37,000 American soldiers were using heroin, a terrible catastrophe from the point of view of the army. And what was more, they were using a new, more potent form of the drug, called heroin no. 4. Heroin no. 3 had traditionally been the strongest form of opium made, but in the late 1960s laboratories in Thailand invented no. 4, which is injected rather than smoked. The invention of no. 4 created an epidemic. Fourteen-year-old girls stood beside the road between Saigon and the U.S. Army base, selling heroin to GI's. Suddenly heroin was everywhere.

American soldiers did something else for the Golden Triangle: they made the taste for its drugs international. GI's back in the United States wanted Thai heroin; soldiers and ex-soldiers still in Vietnam were willing to supply it. Suddenly, incredible amounts of money could be made. The American high command charged that the communists were flooding our soldiers with heroin to weaken their fighting power, but in fact it was our "friends," who were in daily contact with the soldiers, who were supplying the drugs. And the CIA turned out to be a participant, perhaps accidentally, once again. The principal CIA contact in Thailand, chief of police General Phao Sriyanonda, ran the opium trade. In the mid-1960s, according to a highly respected study, *The Politics of Heroin in Southeast Asia*, by Alfred McCoy, General Phao set up a totally corrupt system within the Thai police department. The police guarded the caravans as they came down into the lowlands; the police themselves took the opium to Bangkok, the capital city, loaded it onto boats, and in mid-ocean met freighters that then transferred the drugs to Singapore or Hong Kong; the police even staged phony raids on KMT Army smugglers, in which no opium was taken and no one arrested.

In South Vietnam itself, as thousands of American soldiers were dying, the government we had come to save was responsible for the death of hundreds more. McCoy asserts that the buying and distribution of opium throughout the country was organized through the office of General Nguyen Ngoc Loan, chief of police and security. The entire Vietnamese government floated on a sea of corruption and bribery. It is an iron law of the drug trade that wherever it goes it corrupts governments and police forces. With millions of dollars to be made, it can hardly be otherwise. In especially corrupt countries, the police and government officials begin by cooperating with the drug trade and end up by running it.

In Southwest Asia and Mexico, no one person or small group controls the opium trade; in these lawless areas, neither the government nor anyone else can command obedience. The Golden Triangle, however, is largely ruled by warlords. Several generations ago these people would have been princes, ruling by virtue of nobility. Now they are the people who command the most firepower. Around each of these people an army forms, so that the Golden Triangle is ruled by roving bands of soldiers: the KMT, the Burmese Communist Party, the Shan United Army. The last group is ruled by Khun Sa, a Burmese rebel who is probably the biggest narcotics smuggler in the world. By following his operation we can see how opium gets from the village to the international airport, and we can learn something of the world of the narcotics warlord.

Khun Sa comes from a princely family in the Shan area of northern Burma, an area that has been in open revolt against the Burmese government since 1958. He began smuggling as an officer with the Burmese army in 1963, left to form a private army of his own, and became a minor warlord. The Burmese government paid him off to return to the army, but he left once again with a 2,000-man force of his own. Soon he had made himself the dominant force along the border between Burma and

Thailand, and in 1967 he decided to humble the KMT Army, his biggest challenger. He demanded that the KMT Army pay a tax to pass through "his" territory. The Chinese declared war on the Shans, and caravans from both sides, each carrying tons of opium, met in the battle of Ban-Khwan, in Laos. Meanwhile, though, the government of Laos had learned about the battle, and almost as soon as it started the Laotian air force bombed both sides. When both armies fled, General Ouane Rattikone, chief of the Laotian army, entered the area, took the opium, and thus strengthened his own position as one of the great opium warlords in the Golden Triangle.

Khun Sa's army was in ruins, and he himself was arrested by the Burmese. But his soldiers arranged for his freedom with a kidnap ransom, and he began rebuilding his army. When a rival landlord, Lo Sinh Han, was arrested in 1973, Khun Sa took over his territory, made peace with the KMT and the Burmese Communist Party, and resumed his position as the most powerful of the opium warlords. Like the Pathans, Khun Sa's Shans operate on either side of the border, crossing into Burma when Thai soldiers attack, moving into Thailand when the Burmese send troops after them.

Khun Sa controls perhaps half of the 600 or so tons of opium produced annually in the Golden Triangle. Much of this is consumed in the villages; of the remainder, Khun Sa buys some and receives a tax from others on the rest. One of his agents goes up to the village and bargains with the farmers for a price on their opium. Whatever he pays will be paltry compared with the opium's value to the Shan United Army, though it may sound like a great deal to the poor peasant. The opium is then taken by mule caravan to a point lower down, where it can be boiled until it is half its weight—and twice its strength. Often it is then "cooked" again to make morphine base, still a simple operation. The opium is boiled in an oil drum, over a wood fire, until it dissolves, and then lime fertilizer is added; a combination of chalky water and the dissolved opium rises to the top of the pot. The mixture is strained and boiled again, this time with concentrated ammonia, until the morphine turns solid and drops to the bottom of the pot. Filtered through a cloth again, it leaves white kernels that are morphine base.

Whatever is left—boiled-down opium or morphine base—is loaded on mules and joins a vast caravan of hundreds of soldiers and mules. Some of these caravans stretch a mile or more, and the soldiers are armed to the teeth with mortars, machine guns, recoilless rifles, semiautomatic carbines, and modern radio and communications equipment. The goal of the trip is any of the dozen or so laboratories that Khun Sa maintains along the border to convert opium or morphine base into no. 3 heroin.

The word "laboratory" conjures up the image of a shiny building with glass tubing and aluminum ovens, but a heroin laboratory is nothing more than a bamboo shack with wood, pots, lime, and various chemicals. If soldiers or rivals attack, the laboratory can be abandoned with nothing valuable left behind. But the actual operation that produces heroin is far more difficult than the simple boiling down that occurred earlier, and it requires a chemist with some experience. The essential ingredient is the one that Bayer discovered, acetic anhydride, which greatly increases the strength of the morphine. The morphine must be boiled with acetic anhydride for six hours at 185 degrees, though the cook is more likely to decide when it is ready with his finger than with a thermometer. This new mixture must then be treated with chloroform, boiled with sodium carbonate, purified several times with alcohol and charcoal, combined with hydrochloric acid and ether, filtered, and dried.

The last leg of the trip, so far as Khun Sa or any of the other warlords are concerned, is transporting the no. 3 heroin out of the jungle and into the lowlands area of southern Thailand, where the heroin is sold to representatives of the crime groups operating out of Bangkok or Hong Kong. Some of the heroin is taken farther south to Malaysia, where it is loaded on boats bound for the port cities of Southeast Asia. But much of it is taken only as far as the first big city, a provincial capital called Chiang Mai. Chiang Mai is the sort of city we will be running across throughout this book, a place in between the fields where the drugs are grown and first refined and the major city where the refined drugs are brought to be distributed abroad. It is like Landi Kotal, but far larger and richer.

Many drug smugglers practically live in Chiang Mai, and they have surrounded themselves with luxury. Between 1979 and 1981, according to an American anthropologist, sixteen new hotels were built in this one medium-sized city, though not all of them were constructed with drug money. It is here that people make connections—with Taiwanese criminals, with corrupt Thai officials, even with gangsters from Corsica who stayed in Indochina after World War II. From Chiang Mai or other cities, drugs are sent on to the coast—by tour bus, truck, train, or car—and broken down into small amounts so that a courier can put them in his suitcase before boarding an international flight, or so that they can be put on board boats bound for other major cities.

At first both the Thai and the Burmese governments were reluctant to move against Khun Sa and other warlords, reasoning that they were causing more of a problem for Americans and Europeans than for their own people. That is no longer the case. The tiny nation of Burma now has 35,000 registered heroin addicts (the government itself distributes the drug to official addicts), and possibly three times that number who are unregistered. Thailand is estimated to have between 300,000 and 600,000 heroin addicts, almost as many as the United States, which has five times the population. Since the mid-1970s both countries, working with agents from the U.S. Drug Enforcement Administration, have sent troops into the Golden Triangle. In 1974 some 1,500 Burmese soldiers attacked 400 Shan rebels who were guarding a laboratory near the border. After several hours of fierce battle the Burmese finally drove the rebels out. Around the laboratory they found hundreds of pounds of opium as well as stacks of acetic anhydride and lime, five rocket launchers, five 77-mm. recoilless guns, hundreds of shells, and a pile of bazookas—much of it American equipment from the war.

More recently Thai troops have been staging one battle after another with Khun Sa, none of them totally successful. In the fall of 1981 between 3,000 and 4,000 Thai troops marched against Khun Sa's equally large army and were beaten back. Even when the Thais win, the victory is only temporary. In the spring of 1982 nearly 800 heavily armed members of the Thai Border Patrol Police conducted a secret raid against Khun Sa's border stronghold, Ban Hin Taek. Khun Sa's 2,000 soldiers, roused from their beds and still in their underwear, began blazing away with automatic weapons. After three days and at least seventy deaths, Khun Sa's soldiers fled. When the Thai border police inspected the town, they found that it had tennis courts, a soccer field, fancy shops, and fine homes for the officers and chemists. Khun Sa himself lived in a hilltop mansion with a television set in every room, an elaborate stereo system, and a swimming pool. But the warlord and his staff escaped, sure to re-establish their power.

Khun Sa himself, like the other warlords, claims that he has taken up the opium business as a rebel, not as a criminal. In his own mind he is continuing the long tradition of Shan resistance to the central government. Anthropologist David Feingold has met with Khun Sa several times and claims that "he wants to be the George Washington of the Shan states." On several occasions Khun Sa and other warlords have offered to sell their entire stock of opium to the United States as proof that all they want is enough money to conduct their independence struggle. In 1978 Khun Sa sent a letter to President Jimmy Carter offering to sell to the United States 500 tons of opium over a five-year period for $30 million. The Carter administration decided that trusting warlords is probably a poor idea and pointed out that he could always have more produced if he wanted. So Khun Sa remains public enemy number one in Thailand, whose government has put a $25,000 price tag on his head. Khun Sa is said to have retaliated by offering rewards for the murder of both Thai and foreign narcotics agents in Chiang Mai and by setting up hit squads to get them. So far neither Khun Sa nor the agents have been harmed.

COCAINE

HEROIN IS grown all over the world, but almost the entire supply of cocaine originates on the steep slopes of the Andes mountain range in Bolivia and Peru. The proper conditions of soil and weather might exist elsewhere, but the Andean peasants have been cultivating the coca bush for hundreds of years, and, in any case, they supply more than enough for the cocaine users of South America and the United States. The coca leaf has much the same place among the hardworking farmers on South America's west coast as opium does among the hill tribes of the Golden Triangle. Coca, like opium—like most narcotics—dulls pain, and farmers have always chewed some to make the exhausting work of farming steep mountainsides less burdensome.

Until the late 1960s most farmers in the Andes simply grew the coca bush alongside whatever other crops flourished in the poor soil, on sharp inclines, and in the sometimes dense jungle where they lived. Other bushes, such as coffee and tea, also do well in dry soil, and the farmer would sell these at the nearby market. Much of the coca, however, was consumed within the town or village where he lived. Coca was one crop among many,

South American peasant working his coca field. (DRUG ENFORCEMENT ADMINISTRATION)

The coca plant. The leaf is ground into coca paste. (DRUG ENFORCEMENT ADMINISTRATION)

often grown in a plot that might be as small as your classroom. The Andean peasants lived a poor and simple life, remote from the opportunities as well as the dangers of the city.

Then wealthy Americans developed a taste for cocaine, and everything changed. Men from the city began to come to the little towns at the foot of the mountains and offer to buy the whole town's coca crop. They urged the peasants to devote more and more of their tiny fields to the coca leaf. The supply of cocaine was too small, and the buying agents began to compete with one another and to threaten the peasants to make sure that they would sell only to them. New and even more difficult territory—the "high jungle"—was opened up for coca fields. At the same time, however, government authorities began to come to destroy their coca fields, or at least threaten to do so. The peasants in the mountains of Bolivia and Peru may be slightly less poor than they used to be, but they have also had their peace shattered. At least the warlord system in the Golden Triangle makes the farmer's life easy; the violent competition for control of the Andean cocaine business endangers everyone, starting with the peasant.

But efforts to convince South American farmers to stop growing the coca leaf have proved even less successful than the similar battle against opium in Southeast Asia. Like the hill tribes of the Golden Triangle, the Andean peasants want their drug as much for themselves as to sell to others. Unlike opium, coca can be grown and harvested almost effortlessly, whereas food crops require more work. Those farmers who have stopped growing coca in favor of something else have often been threatened by traffickers and forced to start growing the coca bush once again.

The biggest problem, however, is that the governments of Bolivia and Peru have done little either to destroy coca fields or to provide alternatives to farmers. Peru, on the one hand, is in a situation similar to Thailand or Pakistan: its government is determined to make a dent in the growth of drugs, but it is unwilling to disrupt the lives of farmers or to challenge tradition. Bolivia, on the other hand, is more like Vietnam or Laos in the mid-1960s—a nation controlled by narcotics. Until recently Bolivia had a smuggler's union. The government of Bolivia has resisted almost all attempts to prevent coca from being grown and transported, and American drug officials throw up their hands in disgust when they speak of the country.

The Peruvian government, with American help, has made some effort both to destroy coca and to provide different ways of making a living for the peasants who grow it. Some observers report, however, that when members of the Peruvian Civil Guard enter a village to wipe out its coca crop, they tear up bushes while reporters and photographers watch and then stop when the spectators leave. The bushes, in any case, grow back after a few months. But the best way to stop people from doing something is not simply to punish them but to give them something better to do. American drug officials have realized that merely destroying coca, or telling farmers to grow coffee instead, will not succeed; coca is, after all, an easier crop to grow than coffee. Peasants must feel that they will be more prosperous and healthy if they cooperate with the government than if they cooperate with the smugglers. So the Agency for International Development (AID), along with another branch of the State Department called the Bureau for International Narcotics Matters, has now begun programs for "integrated rural development" in Peru as well as in Thailand. These programs mean that the government won't just offer peasants the seeds for different crops, but will also build roads, schools, and health clinics, allow the farmers to borrow money at low rates, and offer free agricultural advice. Coca gives farmers a chance to earn some extra cash; integrated rural development holds out the promise of a more modern, stable life. The program also helps the government keep an eye on the farmers: with government officials swarming around the countryside, the peasants will have a much harder time secretly growing coca.

American officials in drug enforcement and economic development are cautiously optimistic about the program in Peru. Americans are now working with the Peruvians in the Huallaga Valley, a once-quiet area that turned into a boom town with the explosion of the cocaine business ten years ago. Members of the United States Drug Enforcement Administration (DEA) fear that if programs like this one fail, Peru could eventually become as corrupted with drug money as Bolivia and Colombia now are. And failures are not hard to find. DEA official Dick Webber remembers driving down a $60-million highway built by AID to open up the jungle foothills of Bolivia for development. Half the new road was covered with drying coca leaves. Until AID got there, the area was too dense with vegetation for farming. As soon as the road was built, cocaine smugglers brought farmers into the area and made it a prime source of cocaine.

Once the coca is harvested and dried, a "mule," a representative of a smuggling group, comes to buy it and carry it out. Since small things are easier to hide than big things, a general rule in the drug business is that the original, bulky crop should be cooked down into a smaller, purer form before it leaves the village, though the final process requires special skills and equipment. Coca leaves rarely leave the village unless they are going to the market to be sold legally. In Bolivia and Peru the coca leaf is legal until some foreign substance—one of the chemicals required to make cocaine—is added. The first thing that happens to the leaf is that either the farmer or the mule dumps a load of it into a 55-gallon oil drum. The drum is then lowered into a hole, which is lined with plastic, and the top is covered with kerosene. Inside the warm earth, the leaves begin to dissolve, and after several hours, or even days, form a brown-gray paste with a liquid on top. The liquid is poured off, and the mule has his coca paste.

The peasant is the low man on the totem pole of cocaine money, but the mule is not all that much higher. The mule will pay the farmer perhaps $350 for a kilo of coca paste; since it takes 150 pounds of leaves to make a single kilo of paste, the farmer may sell only a kilo or two. The mule must then wrap the paste in llama skins, load it into a car or truck, and drive it to the laboratory where it will be turned into cocaine base, the next step. This part of the trip is very dangerous, because coca paste has an extremely strong smell, which can be hidden for only so long. The mule may have a short trip or he may have to drive several hundred miles into Colombia, where most of the laboratories are located. If the mule is fully employed by a smuggling ring, he may be paid a tiny salary for his work and for the risk he has taken; otherwise he may receive as much as $2,000 a kilo, but he will have large expenses to pay.

By the time the chemist and the professional smugglers for whom he works receive the coca paste, its value has begun to skyrocket. Coca paste is made into cocaine base, and then into cocaine, in laboratories across South America—in Bolivia and Peru as well as in Argentina and Brazil, but above all in Colombia. Many laboratories are located in big cities like Medellín or Bogotá in Colombia, where traffickers might buy an old warehouse or some other neglected building. In the countryside they might buy a farm, where the coming and going of trucks would not be noticed; finished cocaine can be smuggled out in trucks loaded with produce.

In order to make cocaine base a chemist pours as much as 50 pounds of paste into an iron cauldron, mixes in several acids, and then has the peasants who work for him stir the bubbling paste for hours until it has been reduced by about half. A single kilo of this cocaine base might be worth $10,000 on the open market, but usually the chemist goes on to make cocaine. This is done by washing and straining the base, adding hydrochloric acid, acetone, and finally ordinary household bleach to turn the brown mixture white. The cocaine is then spread into pans and placed in an oven to dry. What emerges are crystallized white chunks. Unlike opium—which is bought and carried out of the fields by one group, picked

Before and after, coca leaf and cocaine crystal. (DRUG
ENFORCEMENT ADMINISTRATION)

up and smuggled out of the country by a second, and sold
in foreign countries by yet a third—cocaine is often controlled from start to finish by the same group. Such a
complex network is hard to organize, but earns the most
money. Just as the peasant gets the least profit, the
people who sell to the users get the most. If the organization made its money selling cocaine to smugglers in Colombia, it might get $20,000 a kilo. But by the time that
kilo gets to the streets of New York its value might be ten
or more times as great. A sophisticated drug ring can
earn close to one thousand times as much on a kilo of
cocaine as it paid the farmer for it.

In a country the size of Bolivia or Colombia drugs are
likely to be the single largest business. Cocaine is estimated to bring $3 billion a year into Colombia, more than
its coffee crop. It might seem, then, that drugs are a good
thing for the country that grows them, as long as the

native population doesn't abuse them, as is the case with Southeast Asian heroin. If we look more closely, though, at what and *whom* that money buys, we might consider cocaine a poor investment indeed.

As of 1982 it was safe to say that Bolivia was the only country in the world that was actually run by drug profiteers. The country's president, General Luis García Meza, who overthrew his democratically elected predecessor, is generally believed to offer protection to Bolivia's top smuggling rings in return for a share of their profits—a charge made in a 1980 Los Angeles *Times* article, and confirmed by DEA agents. His ministers of education and the interior are actually smugglers. The interior minister is reported to use three Piper aircraft and a converted DC-4 to ship vast amounts of cocaine base to Colombia. In Bolivia corruption runs from top to bottom:

A cocaine laboratory, where the paste is boiled, refined, and dried into cocaine. (DRUG ENFORCEMENT ADMINISTRATION)

from the president downward to the local police. No one is going to be punished for smuggling cocaine, or for helping those who do.

How does this happen? The answer is simple: money. In a country as poor as Bolivia, it is not very difficult to bribe a policeman or a member of the local government. And drug smuggling has made a small number of Bolivians fabulously wealthy. With millions of dollars smugglers can bribe cabinet officials. Even better, they can have themselves appointed to the cabinet. Drug smugglers need friends in high places to protect them; in Bolivia, they have gone right to the top. It's easy for them: they have so much more money than anyone else that they have the power to make and break governments.

If the effect of drug money on politics is disastrous, the effect on the economy is just as bad. Politicians elected to further the aims of criminals are not likely to care terribly much about the well-being of their people. Bolivia was one of the poorest countries in South America before the smugglers gained power, but things can only get worse now. With so much coca being planted, Bolivia is now suffering a shortage of its traditional crops—rice, corn, and yucca. And even all the money that smugglers earn brings the country no prosperity. For money to improve people's well-being it must be invested in some sort of useful work—for example, in companies that make the things consumers need or that employ many people.

Poor countries like Bolivia have special needs of their own: they need roads and bridges, schools and hospitals, modern farming equipment, ordinary consumer goods.

But drug smugglers, of course, don't invest their money in their native country; they spend it on Mercedes cars and fancy apartments, not to mention bribery. They ship much of their loot abroad, where it fills the banks, and in this country they buy the best real estate in southern Florida. They don't even spend money to improve the farming on which they depend. Coca can be grown and harvested in plenty without modern techniques, and smugglers, in any case, don't want the farmers to get too prosperous and independent; they might go into business for themselves. What drug money does to a country can be seen, in miniature, in Tingo Maria, Peru, the smugglers' own capital, the Chiang Mai or Landi Kotal of cocaine. This little town has only one paved road, and its population consists largely of poor peasants. But its one road has six banks and a string of auto dealerships that sell cars for cash. The city government is controlled by the smugglers' party.

Colombia is even more nearly saturated with cocaine money than Bolivia is. Very little cocaine is grown there, but Colombians have dominated international cocaine smuggling from the beginning. Most coca paste and cocaine base are refined into cocaine in Colombia, and a large part of the 25 to 30 tons of cocaine consumed in the United States arrives aboard flights from Colombia's capital, Bogotá.

The Colombian government has made serious efforts to wipe out the cocaine trade, but it is a lonely struggle. Cocaine is estimated to support 100,000 families, a very large proportion of the country's 18 million people. Corruption is routine among policemen, soldiers, judges, government officials, and others in positions of authority.

High government officers are found leaving the country with cocaine in their suitcases. The national air force is used to transport cocaine. Drug enforcement agents are terrorized: in February 1982, two agents from the DEA were kidnapped from a hotel room in Cartagena, a port city, hauled out to the jungle, shot, and left for dead. (They both survived.) Periodically the government sends federal police into the countryside to destroy part of the small coca crop, and occasionally it succeeds in arresting a major trafficker, but the government is no match for the smugglers.

MARIJUANA

MARIJUANA IS a weed; it grows all over. These days it is mostly grown on purpose, as a way of making money, but it still grows wild in various parts of the United States, especially the Midwest. Until early in this century marijuana was legally cultivated in the United States and elsewhere as a source of hemp. The hollow stem of the plant is ideal for rope, and thus the plant used to be known as Indian hemp. But people have also known about its narcotic use for centuries. An ancient Greek historian writes of the practice of roasting marijuana seeds and sniffing the fumes. In South and Central America and the Middle East, where most marijuana has traditionally been grown, it is smoked to dull pain and give mild pleasure, like coca and opium; like them it has also been connected to ancient religious rituals.

The tall, spiky marijuana plant. (DRUG ENFORCEMENT ADMINISTRATION)

Only in the last fifteen years has marijuana become popular outside these areas, and only since the mid-1970s or so has it been so widely and casually used that it can be spoken of as a "recreational drug." This explosion in popularity—every year Americans smoke something like 10,000 tons of marijuana, worth roughly $20 billion—has completely changed the first stage of the marijuana business, the growing process and the first leg of smuggling. Areas such as Jamaica, which used to grow large quantities of marijuana, have been sharply cut down through enforcement measures. Other areas, such as California and Colombia, where the marijuana crop was not taken so seriously, have increased production. And the whole business of growing and smuggling, once done in a rather casual way by unconnected individuals, has now become a highly sophisticated, well-organized, and dangerous business. As Florida Senator Lawton Chiles told a congressional committee: "I think we have to forget the image of marijuana as a couple of giggling teenagers behind the high school gymnasium smoking a joint. We are talking about cold-blooded killers, organized crime, an international operation which floats billions from bank to bank around the world." We will look at marijuana in three places where it is grown: Mexico, California, and Colombia.

MEXICO

Much of the western coast of Mexico is hot, dry, and mountainous, bad for farming but good for banditry and drugs. The area has not been in rebellion, at least not for the last sixty years, but it has been controlled largely by a local Mafia. One region, Durango, has been under the domination of a single family, the Herreras, for generations. The Herreras have supervised the growing and smuggling of both marijuana and opium, as well as other illegal businesses, like gambling and prostitution, which generally attract organized crime. Until recently almost all of America's marijuana and a large part of its heroin came from this coastal region. Now much of the drug crop has been wiped out—and this, too, is part of our story.

Mexican farmers used to grow marijuana, as often as not, by throwing seeds into the ground and harvesting whatever came up. A marijuana plant can grow as high as 12 feet with relatively little encouragement, as long as the rainfall is adequate. It was normal to plant in May or

June, just before the rainy season, so that moisture was not a problem. When American buyers began coming in the 1960s, however, demanding higher quality marijuana and more of it, the farmers began cultivating more carefully.

In Mexico marijuana is grown in dry soil on hillsides, like the coca bush in the Andes. Not only does the plant grow well in these conditions, but it is easier to hide from the police in the remote mountains than on the plains. Because farmers grow the crop on steep hillsides, they often terrace their plots—that is, they build steps into the hill, each step perhaps two feet deep, so that the plants can grow on a flat surface. Seeds are planted in rows along each step. As the plants come up, the farmers often build little dikes around them to hold the water, which the farmers must provide. If they plant a second crop in October, after the rainy season, this step is crucial. Several times a week the farmer must walk among the plants and pluck off the lower leaves, which consume much of the nutrition but provide little THC, or tetrahydrocannabinol, the ingredient that makes marijuana a drug rather than just a weed. After a month the plants should already be three feet tall. After six months, one week or so after the plant blossoms, it will be about eight feet tall and ready to harvest.

The harvest itself is the most complicated part of the preparation of marijuana. The flowery tips called colas, which contain the most THC, must be picked first. Then as the plant itself is harvested, the leaves from the top half must be separated from those at the bottom, since the THC content is higher toward the top of the plant. Thereafter, though, very little has to be done to

Marijuana and poppy field in Mexico, discovered by drug enforcement troops. (DRUG ENFORCEMENT ADMINISTRATION)

marijuana to make it ready for smoking. There is no chemical difference between "raw" marijuana in the fields and refined marijuana sold to users, as there is between opium and heroin or between coca and cocaine. The leaves and colas must be dried for about ten days and sometimes picked clean of stems and seeds, but that's about it. Sometimes the marijuana is pressed into kilo-sized "bricks" to make it easier to carry, but often it is bundled up in bulk.

Since there is no need for laboratories and chemists, and also because it is too bulky to hide easily, marijuana is not dispensed from a few central points in or near cities, as are heroin and cocaine. Once it is harvested, the marijuana is normally taken out of the field by a pack of mules, heavily escorted by *pistoleros*, or gun-toting guards. Mexicans in this area, like Pathans, carry guns as routinely as they wear sombreros. Armed bandits prowl the mountains looking for opportunities, and the mule train provides a tempting prospect. Usually the mules carry the bales of marijuana down to a plane that has landed on a tiny airstrip, a clearing in the jungle of the lower hills. The pilot then takes off, the plane dipping from hundreds of pounds of new cargo, and flies off to the lowlands. There the plane will be met by marijuana buyers in cars or trucks. They will then be responsible for driving their stash across the border into the United States.

In the early 1970s about three-quarters of American marijuana came from Mexico; by 1979 the figure was down to 10 percent. What happened in between was that Mexico, with help from the United States, conducted a fierce campaign against both marijuana and opium. The fact that this effort succeeded, where so many others have not, may contain some important clues in the war against drugs; as DEA operations chief Abraham Azzam says, "The closer to the source you get, the more effective you are."

Until the mid-1970s the Mexicans viewed marijuana and opium abuse as a strictly American problem, though there were Mexican users. Then vast amounts of oil were discovered in Mexico, and the country embarked on an ambitious development program. Suddenly, as the country looked toward a modern, industrialized future, the underworld of *bandidos, pistoleros*, and smugglers seemed like a gigantic eyesore; and, what was worse, drug money would be an obstacle to development and a source of corruption. So the Mexican government decided, for its own reasons, not because of American pressure, to go after the drug business.

Second, the Mexican government had the ability to reach into the drug world. Throughout most of this century Mexico has had a stable political system and a relatively strong central government, unlike almost all of the other countries we have been talking about. Mexico has a long outlaw tradition, but the government has for a long time been the most powerful force in the country. Moreover, the anti-drug effort would not be ruined from within; the country's leaders and judges were not puppets of the drug trade.

Finally, the government developed a workable program with the DEA. If it had sent troops or the police into remote villages to pull up the crops, as happens elsewhere, the government would have been able to destroy only a small portion of the marijuana and opium fields. Instead, the crops were destroyed with chemicals released from planes. First, the planes flew over the drug-producing areas with special photographic equipment that could distinguish between crops in tiny fields, and then those areas in which marijuana or opium were growing were sprayed. This later caused a furor in the United States, however, because the marijuana was sprayed with an herbicide called paraquat, which did not destroy it but made it poisonous. The crop was harvested and smuggled across the border, reportedly causing serious illness among Americans who used it. For a number of years Congress refused to approve the use of paraquat in drug eradication efforts, but it was resumed in 1979.

The crop eradication effort, like all forms of drug enforcement, has forced the people who benefit from drugs to be more and more clever. Now marijuana and opium are frequently grown in the shadows underneath a cliff, invisible from above. Mexican farmers have invented a whole series of dodges to elude detection. Marijuana and opium plants are often mixed with other crops, so that an aerial photograph will show only corn or beans. This concealment is rather difficult to accomplish with marijuana, however, since it grows so high; so farmers often harvest their marijuana while it is still small. Every time the Mexican authorities detect one trick, the farmers invent a new one. Heroin production has begun to increase once again. But Mexico still has the most successful crop destruction program in the world today. And one final reason for its success has been that the Mexican government has devoted itself to providing peasants a better alternative. Though agricultural development has traditionally been ignored in favor of big industries, the government has now reversed that trend and is spending hundreds of millions of dollars on integrated rural development programs.

CALIFORNIA

Only a small portion of the marijuana smoked in the United States is also grown here, and the domestic variety is not especially prized: American marijuana has a THC content of .2 to 2 percent whereas Colombian marijuana has 6 to 10 percent THC. Growers in California have gotten around this problem by producing a variety known as sinsemilla (the word means "seedless" in Spanish), which may be ten times as strong as ordinary marijuana. Sinsemilla, accordingly, is far more expensive than almost any of its competitors—as much as $3,000 a pound wholesale, maybe twice that on the street.

California probably has the wealthiest drug farmers in the world. Elsewhere all the profit goes to the smugglers, but a grower in Humboldt County, in northern California, can easily sell a crop without much extra help. Many farmers are civil servants or businessmen who grow marijuana in a tiny patch in their back yard. A miniature plot can produce a crop worth as much as $30,000 a year. A story is told of a widow on social security who raised thirteen plants and cleared $8,000. An increasing number of professional growers have also moved into the area, with planes and criminal connections, buying plots of several acres in the woods. But almost all of them use the most modern farming techniques: cross-breeding, irrigation, heavy doses of fertilizer.

Only recently have the police begun to catch up with the farmers, sending spotter planes overhead to pick out the marijuana in the midst of the forest. Much of it is grown in roadless areas, however, and once they approach on the ground the police often find it impossible to locate what they saw from the air. The police also have trouble getting cooperation. Most local citizens don't especially disapprove of marijuana and aren't inclined to aid in the arrest of their neighbors. Local governments are also unenthusiastic, sometimes refusing to accept money for crop destruction programs. And it's not hard to see why: sinsemilla means as much to the economy of northern California as cocaine does to Peru. Marijuana is Humboldt County's leading crop, with an estimated value, in 1979, of $90 million. It is, in fact, more important to California's economy than lettuce or oranges; the state grows as much as a billion dollars' worth of marijuana a year. We have already seen how impoverished countries can come to rely on big money from the drug trade; wealthy areas, it turns out, may do the same thing.

COLOMBIA

There is no greater proof of the power and flexibility of drug smugglers than the fact that in the mid-1970s Colombia was providing a small fraction of America's marijuana, but by 1979 was supplying three-quarters of the total amount. When the squeeze was applied in Mexico, marijuana appeared in Colombia (and opium appeared in Pakistan). The most conservative estimate is that Colombia grows 15,000 tons of marijuana a year; a likelier figure is twice that much. At least 7,000 tons of the Colombian crop make it to American shores. Between 100,000 and 200,000 acres of Colombian land are devoted to the growing of marijuana.

Most of this land has traditionally been in Guajira province, a coastal area on the Atlantic Ocean that is home to one of the world's greatest concentrations of smugglers, narcotic and otherwise. The Colombian police, however, have pinpointed Guajira for their crop destruction effort, uprooting plants, intercepting boats, waiting at deserted airstrips for smugglers' planes to touch down. The growing has thus shifted away from the coast, where it can be easily brought to waiting boats, to the mountainous areas inland, the same Sierra Madres whose slopes the Mexican farmers terrace for their marijuana. Most Colombian marijuana, like cocaine in Peru or Bolivia, is farmed in tiny plots in primitive style. The crop is then purchased by a local organization, loaded onto mules, and taken to the nearest road, where it is placed in a truck. The truck then takes it to storage near a loading area, where it is inspected by interested smugglers, purchased, baled, and finally taken either to a beach or to an airstrip to be carried out of the country.

The Colombian government has reported seizing gigantic quantities of marijuana. In the fall of 1981 the police officer in charge of the national drug squad claimed that his men had been intercepting an average of 80 tons a week. Yet so far the seizures have made no difference. The country produces so much more marijuana than it uses itself that even if large quantities don't make it out of the country there's still plenty left.

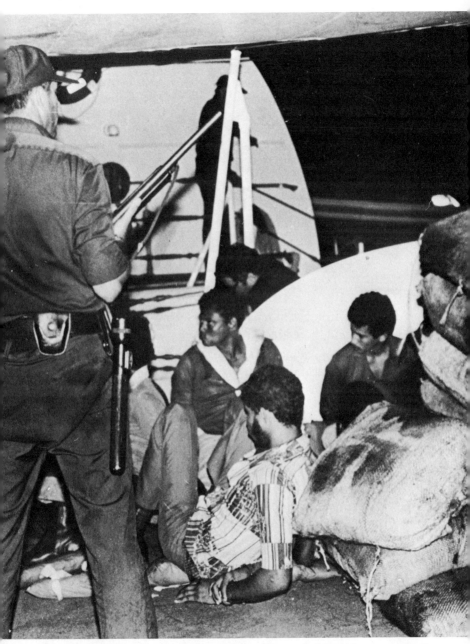

The Columbian crew of a shrimp boat under armed guard near part of the cargo of more than seven tons of marijuana found on board the boat.
(WIDE WORLD PHOTOS)

Marijuana also has a less popular but far more potent cousin—hashish, which is made from a resin that can be scraped off the blossoms of marijuana bushes. It usually has more THC than even the strongest ordinary marijuana; a superconcentrated version, hash oil, can be 60 percent THC. But since hashish is produced mostly in North Africa and the Middle East rather than in Mexico, Jamaica, or Colombia, it is far more popular in Europe than in the United States. Only about 200 tons of hashish are consumed in the United States every year.

The world's largest source of hashish is the Bekaa Valley, the mountainous spine of Lebanon. In 1981 the farmers of the Bekaa grew about 2,000 tons of hashish. Like Afghanistan or Burma, Lebanon is a country in far too much turmoil to be able to control what goes on within its own borders. Since 1975 Lebanon has been torn to shreds by several different wars running simultaneously: Christians battle Moslems; Christian clans battle one another; Arab terrorists fight with one another. Recently the Israelis attacked the Palestinian Liberation Organization as well as a Syrian peacekeeping force. In this chaotic situation Lebanon has been largely run by clans, families with private armies, like the warlords of the Golden Triangle. Many of these clans own rocket launchers, automatic weapons, and even tanks, and some twenty of them control the hashish trade. Prior to the civil war only about 10 percent of the Upper Bekaa Valley's land was used for hashish; now the figure is closer to 80 percent. At one time hashish smugglers used their own private airport; now they send heavily guarded truckloads to the northern coast, where they leave from ports controlled by one of the Christian militias.

Baalbek, the major city of the Bekaa, is another gold-rush town, like Tingo Maria or Chiang Mai. Mercedes and Jaguars, many of them stolen from the streets of Beirut, the nation's capital, cruise up and down the smoothly paved roads; new stone homes have replaced old ones of mud; new factories, businesses, schools, and hospitals have sprung up. The farmers themselves, in an unusual twist, are getting rich, building houses, and sending their children to the university. Townspeople have no more objection to hashish than do the citizens of Humboldt County to sinsemilla. Their crop has probably brought $500 million to the Bekaa. In Lebanon these days there is no such thing as enforcement, and efforts to substitute new crops like sunflowers have not persuaded anyone. Nobody has yet come up with a legal crop that buys Mercedes and Jaguars.

II
SMUGGLING FROM BORDER TO BORDER

HEROIN

THE PROCESS of getting heroin or opium out of the country where it is grown and into the country where it will be used is (even) more complicated and dangerous than the process of growing it, refining it, and bringing it to the border. Far more money is involved. A kilo of heroin can be purchased in Thailand for roughly $10,000 and sold in New York for as much as $200,000. Far more police officials, and better-equipped ones, must be hoodwinked or bribed; there are border police and customs agents at either end, and in whatever country in between that the heroin or opium must pass through. And since there are many more steps in the process, it is easier for something to go wrong.

In getting from Pakistan, Thailand, and Mexico to the United States and Europe the enormous tonnage of opium and heroin crisscrosses the entire globe, including such out-of-the-way places as China, Australia, and South America. Often a small shipment of heroin will be sent back and forth on plane flights over thousands of miles, costing thousands of dollars, in order to fool the police. Traffickers will spend any amount of money to ensure that their packages arrive safely, because success is worth millions to them. And they will kill if need be. The people who control the heroin traffic—or the cocaine or marijuana traffic—do not let human life stand in their way. Nor can they offer a political reason for their violence. There are no liberation struggles among international smugglers.

Only the Mexicans have a relatively easy time of it. A "mule" carrying heroin in his secondhand pickup truck has only to cross somewhere along the 2,000-mile border between northern Mexico and the southwestern United States, and there are thousands of miles of highway to choose from. For this reason we won't talk about Mexican heroin smuggling, though a constant battle of wits is being waged between Mexican traffickers and the American Border Patrol. Instead we will begin with a brief description of Southeast Asian heroin and then discuss at length the long trek of Southwest Asian heroin across Central Asia, Eastern Europe, Western Europe, and finally on to the United States.

SOUTHEAST ASIA

When opium reaches the Southeast Asian port cities of Bangkok, Hong Kong, Kuala Lumpur, and so forth, it generally falls under the control of Chinese gangs known as Triads, often called the Chinese Mafia. These super-secret organizations exist in many cities with a large Chinese population all over the world. There are said to be thirty-three Triad societies with eighty thousand members. An ancient ritual is still used to swear in the rare new member; once in, the newcomer must keep utter secrecy about the group's activities, which include not only drug smuggling but gambling, prostitution, and ex-tortion. In Hong Kong, where they are centered, the Triads control every aspect of the city's criminal life. Unlike the Mafia, however, the Triads are not dominated by the heads of a few families. Each Triad is independent and works with the others. Thus a Triad-controlled labo-ratory in Kuala Lumpur, in Malaysia, might convert morphine to heroin, and gang members might then place the heroin on a boat headed for Bangkok. There mem-bers of another Triad might unload the heroin, place it in a suitcase, and turn it over to a courier, who might fly to Australia, then to South Korea, and then to Amsterdam. There the courier would deliver the cargo to yet another Triad Society, which would be responsible for selling the opium in Europe.

During the 1970s Amsterdam was, in fact, the favorite drop-off spot for Chinese gangs peddling heroin in Europe. At that time Holland's drug laws were so soft that a Chinese trafficker caught with thirteen kilos of heroin—that's eight million nickel bags (enough for one use), as we counted it earlier—was sentenced to only three months in prison. Toward the end of the decade, though, the Chinese started getting crowded out by the cheap and plentiful heroin from Southwest Asia. In a matter of weeks twenty-six heroin users in Amsterdam died after using Southwest Asian heroin. The police speculated that local Chinese had poisoned a batch of the rival heroin on orders from the dealers who controlled the Southeast Asian trade. The charge was never proved, but it illustrates how closely the Chinese community in a city abroad works with the dealers from overseas.

The secrecy and cooperation within the Triad Societies, and within the larger Chinese communities, have made it practically impossible to break the international connection on which heroin from Southeast Asia depends. When the police try to place a Chinese undercover agent inside a Triad, he is questioned endlessly about his parents, his hometown, his friends. If he slips up and reveals that he is lying, he is immediately executed. But this same secrecy has made it difficult for the Chinese to sell the heroin that they smuggle. The Chinese in the United States and Europe do not know the people who normally sell heroin. Because the Chinese live in their own neighborhoods almost everywhere they go, often working and educating their children separately from the rest of the society, they have difficulty plugging into the drug network. Smugglers in Bangkok or Hong Kong are often desperate for contacts abroad.

This, police have found, is their soft spot. Narcotics agents have been able to recruit local Chinese to help them by posing as drug sellers or mobsters, thus luring the big trafficker here in order to make arrangements.

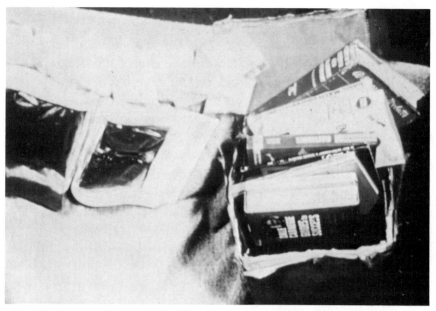

Drugs are often smuggled into the country in hollowed-out books or suitcases. (DRUG ENFORCEMENT ADMINISTRATION)

This tactic was used in one of the biggest busts ever, the arrest of chemist Li Kin Wah and eight other major heroin distributors, along with 183 pounds of heroin—enough to supply all American users for about ten days. The DEA recruited a travel agent formerly from Hong Kong, Charlie Wu, to make contacts with New York's heroin underworld. Before long a woman from Hong Kong offered to Wu and his "boss"—a DEA agent named Robert Allen—as much heroin as they wanted. As proof she sent a can of tea containing 1.2 grams of 95 percent pure heroin to a Manhattan post office box. Allen offered to buy more.

After over a year of waiting Allen finally got a phone call from Li, who wanted to do business. Li had known

Charlie Wu in Hong Kong and thus was convinced that Allen could be trusted. Allen then went to Bangkok, where he convinced Li to buy no. 3 heroin with him and then to go to New York where he could process it into no. 4 at Allen's own laboratory (which he actually built). Li arrived in New York, where Allen set him up, and called one of his friends in Thailand to send over twenty-six pounds of heroin. When the man arrived, both he and Li were arrested. Wu then arranged another meeting in Hong Kong with Li's big distributor, William Chen, and persuaded Chen to come to New York to meet Allen's "boss," Joe Q—another DEA agent. Chen himself, along with others in his gang, was arrested soon after Chen met with Joe Q at an Italian restaurant and spoke openly of his criminal activities.

SOUTHWEST ASIA

The principal problem facing Chinese drug traffickers is finding an outlet through which to sell the drugs that they smuggle; for those working the Golden Crescent—the area spanning Pakistan, Afghanistan, and Iran—the greatest difficulty is transporting the opium or heroin to Western Europe and the United States. The Chinese gangsters, on the one hand, have their highly efficient laboratories in the same countries in which the opium grows; all they have to do is load it on a plane headed for its final destination. And they have a single ruthlessly efficient organization, or group of organizations, doing business with one another around the world. Southwest

Asia, on the other hand, does not—at least not yet—have sophisticated laboratories in which to produce no. 4 heroin. Some heroin is produced in Pakistan and sent directly to Europe and the United States, but addicts do not buy it if they have a choice. This means that the opium—or sometimes the morphine base—must be sent to the laboratories. And the best laboratories and chemists are now in Sicily, the island south of Italy. This is a very long journey, and it cannot be made by plane because the opium is far too bulky. What this means is that Southwest Asian heroin, unlike that from Southeast Asia, must travel great distances over land and pass through many hands on its way to the United States or Western Europe. It is a journey as amazing, in its own way, as the endless caravans of silks and spices that crossed the plains of Asia and the forests and rivers of Europe centuries ago.

The trip generally begins in Pakistan since, as we mentioned earlier, that is where most of the opium available for export is grown. Some of this opium will be converted within the North-West Frontier Province to morphine base, or even heroin, and taken to Karachi to be put aboard a plane. Almost all of this cargo will be taken aboard Pakistani International Airlines, the government airline, often by stewards or even pilots. The Pakistani government has fought a running war against corruption in its own airline, on one occasion firing much of the staff. Most of the opium, though, either stays up north to be carried across Afghanistan or is taken to southern Pakistan, which borders on Iran. The outbreak of war in Afghanistan has made the second choice a good deal more common.

If it remains in the form of opium, the drug is usually loaded into trucks or packed on mules; morphine, being much lighter, is often carried in cars. Immense quantities of opium are often involved. In March 1980, for instance, the Pakistani government stopped an oil truck carrying 7,000 pounds of opium—enough to last American addicts a month if converted to heroin. By now, and for the next several thousand miles, the smugglers are Kurds, members of the nomadic tribe that has been peddling goods, legal and illegal, across Asia for a thousand years. The Kurds, at one time or another, have made war with the governments of most of the countries they pass through, so they are often not bothered. Presently, for example, the Kurds are in virtual revolt against the Iranian government, and northern Iran, their homeland, is under Kurdish control. Afghanistan, however, is another story. It seems amazing that opium, or anything else, is smuggled across Afghanistan. Most of the country's few roads are controlled by the Russian or Afghan armies, which are fighting against rebel soldiers. Smugglers are natural allies of the rebels, who often sell opium in order to buy guns. Yet the caravans continue to pass through, probably at night, with the opium concealed under a load of dried fruit or nuts. Of course, the Kurds don't always use the roads. With their mules or camels they can walk the hundreds of miles across the high planes of Afghanistan, which are freezing in winter and barren in summer.

The Iranian Revolution has left that country, too, in a state of confusion, a fact which, as usual, has been exploited by the smugglers. The mullahs, or clergymen, who now control Iran have punished almost all crimes severely, but none more so than drug smuggling. The widespread drug addiction in the country is considered a grave violation of Islamic law, and the mullahs have tried to root it out pitilessly. In a single day in May of 1980 twenty drug dealers were said to have been executed by firing squad. Yet even as the punishment grows more harsh, the opportunities to earn money from drugs grow greater. Illegal activity has increased in Iran as many different factions contend for power, and yet none possess it completely. Families trying desperately to leave the country have found that one way of raising money is by selling heroin.

This has produced a whole new class of smugglers, young men who board a plane in Teheran, the capital, with a kilo or two of heroin to sell in Europe or the United States. Most of them are amateurs, acting independently of one another, but already they have developed their own methods. Many Iranians seem to believe that packages will never be opened in the United States, and thus they send heroin through the mail. Others place the drug in luggage without identification and then try to claim it in the United States. A group of Iranians living in California sent opium through the mail in the frames of mounted photographs of Ayatollah Khomeini, the country's spiritual leader. Police found a dozen of these photographs containing 16 kilos of opium. In another case, police found an Iranian trying to sneak 4.5 kilos of heroin into Chicago's O'Hare airport in twenty cans of Iranian black caviar. Federal narcotics officials are beginning to fear that an Iranian connection may be forming.

But Iran still serves mainly as a transit point for opium

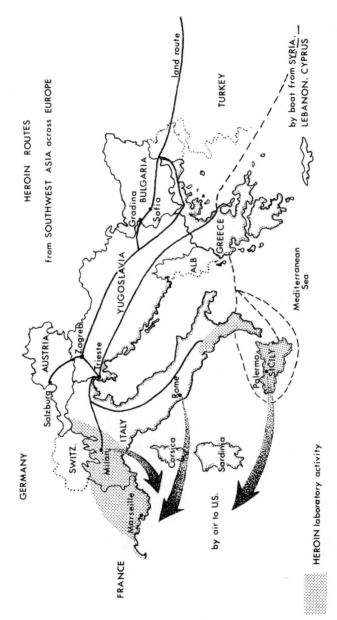

HEROIN ROUTES

from SOUTHWEST ASIA across EUROPE

land route

by boat from SYRIA, LEBANON, CYPRUS

GERMANY

AUSTRIA

Salzburg

SWITZ.

Milan

FRANCE

Marseille

ITALY

Corsica

Sardinia

Zagreb

Trieste

YUGOSLAVIA

Rome

Gradina

Sofia

BULGARIA

TURKEY

ALB

GREECE

Palermo

SICILY

Mediterranean Sea

by air to U.S.

HEROIN laboratory activity

crossing from Pakistan to Turkey and beyond. At its far northwestern corner—all the way across, from the point of view of the Kurd coming from Pakistan—Iran borders on Turkey, and it is there that most caravans head in order to drop off their opium and have it converted into morphine base. A few laboratories are on the Iranian side of the border, but most are in Turkey, especially in the eastern cities of Diyarbakir and Gaziantep. These cities are normally the end of the line for the Kurds, who have traveled as much as 3,000 miles, through deserts as well as over mountains, with their cargo.

They are, however, the beginning of the line for the Turkish connection, which the heroin trade has never been able to do without. This is in part owing to Turkey's geographical position as a sort of belt buckle between Europe and Asia. Turkey is both European and Asian, and at times it has been a power on both continents. It has long traded, both in goods and in people, to both its east and its west. And heroin has been part of that trade throughout this century.

The United States first asked Turkey to attempt a crop substitution program in 1923; the government refused, and within a decade Turkey had become the center of the heroin trade. Mafia dons like Lucky Luciano decided that Turkey would be the perfect base for the drug business: the government did little to prevent the growth of poppies, and the opium could be easily loaded on boats bound for Lebanon or Syria. There it was converted to morphine base before going on to southern France for refinement into heroin. Gradually, the Turks edged out the Lebanese and Syrians and began producing morphine base themselves and sending it overland to Europe. This began a pattern that continues to this day, though the opium now comes from the east.

Turkey's reign as the world's leading supplier of opium came to an abrupt end in the early 1970s with two different events. First, the French and French-Corsican mobsters who had organized the entire trade and run the laboratories in Marseille were arrested and their laboratories shut down in the famous police case known as the French connection. Second, the Turkish government finally agreed to ban the growth of poppies and succeeded in limiting their cultivation to what could be used for legal purposes. But if Turkey's first function—the supply of opium—had been lost, its other two—refining it and sending it on to Europe—remained. All that was needed was a source of opium. And this, of course, was provided by Pakistan.

Just as some heroin goes directly from Iran and Pakistan to the United States and Europe, so some goes directly from Turkey to the United States. Turkish smugglers have made a connection with members of organized crime in the eastern United States and have been sending some heroin aboard Turkish ships to U.S. ports. One smuggler is known to have transferred at least 400 pounds of heroin, over several trips, in this manner. A far larger quantity of morphine base and heroin leaves Turkey by boat, skirts through the Mediterranean to the island of Cyprus, and then goes on to Sicily. But most of the morphine or heroin is taken across Turkey to the western city of Istanbul and then sent on into Europe. This, too, is a long trip, but by now we have left the camels and mule trains of Central Asia behind. From now on, the drugs will be moving along highways.

Turkey's great contribution to the drug trade is neither the Kurds who bring the drugs in nor the eastern laboratories which refine them, but the vast numbers of Turkish citizens who regularly surge back and forth between their birthplace and Europe, and who carry the drugs westward. Thirty years ago the sight of a Turk in many cities of Europe would have been remarkable. In the last few decades, though, millions of "guest workers" have streamed northward from southern Europe and westward from Turkey and Asia, leaving their impoverished homes for jobs in prosperous countries that need more workers for occupations like construction or service. They are called guest workers because they are expected to leave when they are no longer needed, and many return frequently to their home and family. Fully a million Turks work in Germany. Many of them return home on vacation, real or invented, and stop off at one of the laboratory towns in the East. There they hide a few kilos of morphine or heroin in a special panel built into their car or truck, and begin the long drive back to Western Europe with a sure source of profit if they can make it. The Turkish guest workers, then, are the third "tribe" carrying Southwest Asian opium along its route: first the Pathans, then the Kurds, and then the Turks. But not all the Turks involved are poor migrants. In 1979 police arrested a former member of Turkey's national assembly named Halit Kharaman, who said that the country's former deputy prime minister had recommended he transport heroin as a way of raising money. Kharaman was clearing $10,000 a kilo.

The trick for the heroin couriers is to avoid inspection at the many borders through which they must pass on their way to Western Europe. One way of doing this is to carry the heroin in what is called a Transport International Routier (TIR) truck. TIR is the result of an agreement among most European and some Asian countries; it requires that cargo be inspected at its point of origin but permitted to pass through borders unexamined.

For couriers traveling by car, however, the first border that they must face is the one separating Turkey from Bulgaria. Since three-quarters of Golden Crescent morphine passes through this border, you would expect the Bulgarian customs officials to conduct a thorough search, checking underneath the car, tapping for hidden panels, questioning the driver and passengers. So far as anyone can tell, however, they don't. Bulgaria is considered a smuggler's paradise. Though Bulgaria is a communist country that serves as a gateway to the noncommunist world, Bulgaria is probably not trying to addict the capitalists. Its customs officials simply have been corrupted, as have so many others involved in drug trafficking. In a system described by a group of investigative reporters in *The Heroin Trail*, the customs agency, KINTEX, seems to work hand in glove with the smugglers. The system, according to a smuggler who spoke to a team of reporters, works as follows. The smuggler "sends a message to Sofia [Bulgaria's capital] giving a description and license number of his truck or car. He also tells what time the truck is expected to cross the border. Then KINTEX sends a man to the crossing point to make sure that the truck gets through without any search." It has also been alleged that KINTEX is an arm of Bulgarian intelligence and supplies weapons to Kurdish revolutionaries and others in exchange for heroin. Guns and heroin, as we have seen, are tangled together all over the world.

The next border is that of Yugoslavia, and the contrast is a stark one. The Yugoslavs take drug enforcement very seriously. One-third of all European seizures of Southwest Asian heroin occur at Gradina, the Yugoslav town that stands on the Bulgarian border. For this reason smugglers have increasingly detoured southward from Bulgaria through Greece, where the border check is more lax. Heroin that has taken a southern route—refined in laboratories in Syria, Iraq, and Lebanon—also arrives in Greece via ferry.

By this time the opium, morphine, or heroin will have passed through six or seven countries and as many border checks. Police seize as much as 1,000 kilos every year, but they probably stop no more than 10 percent of the total amount of drugs, if that. With well over a million cars and trucks passing every year across the vast span of roads connecting Asia to Western Europe, customs officials simply cannot keep up. And the combination of corruption and the ingenuity of smugglers makes it even more difficult to stop the flow of drugs.

The drugs that are intended for users and addicts in Europe have already been refined into heroin, and now spread out across the Continent. The rise of Golden Crescent heroin has been a far greater disaster so far for Europeans than for Americans. Simply because Europe is closer to the source, the heroin there is much cheaper and stronger. Germany had almost no addiction problem in the early 1970s; by 1980 the country had as many as eighty thousand addicts. In 1979 in Germany 616 addicts died from overdoses, almost as many as in the United States, which has many more addicts. Young addicts can now be seen wandering around the big cities of all the major European countries. And no wonder: in the United States an average kilo might sell for $170,000 and be only 3.5 percent pure, while in West Germany or elsewhere in Europe it might cost as little as $24,000 and be 20 percent pure. Southeast Asian heroin, which has almost disappeared from the streets, was never this plentiful or potent.

While the heroin that has been refined in Asia goes north to European users, most of the morphine, intended for the United States, heads south for Italy. This is perhaps the most frightening recent development in the entire world of narcotics trafficking. The Sicilian Mafia, as we mentioned earlier, working with Corsican gangsters (Corsica is a Mediterranean island possession of France) practically invented the modern heroin trade. But during the late 1960s and early 1970s many of these mobsters—Sicilians, Corsicans, French, and Americans—were either killed or arrested. The various French connection cases were thought to have finally destroyed the network of Corsican mobsters and French chemists. The Sicilian Mafia families, both in the United States and Italy, were thought to have dropped out of the heroin business for fear of arrest. It is clear that all of these groups, and above all the Sicilian Mafia, have returned to the heroin business. The Mafia, of course, runs the most sophisticated, dangerous, and violent smuggling operation in the world; and with new laboratories being built in Sicily, northern Italy, and southern France, it has the capacity to turn the huge new supply of opium from the Golden Crescent into heroin bound for the United States.

The return of the Sicilian Mafia to the heroin trade has provoked a bloody war between the gangs and Italian narcotics enforcement authorities. The war began in June 1979, when Sicilian police, after an eight-month investigation along with the DEA, seized $500,000 in cash intended for drug purchases at the airport in Palermo, Sicily's principal city. The next month the police arrested two major Sicilian traffickers. The Mafia struck back by murdering their greatest local enemy, sixty-four-year-old Boris Guiliano, the city's deputy police chief. Earlier the group had murdered one of the city's chief judges and the president of the regional government. Clearly the Mafia is trying to terrify enforcement officials to prevent them from looking any closer. It has not succeeded.

What the police have found is a growing number of laboratories, sometimes staffed by the same French chemists who worked out of Marseille in the 1960s and who disappeared after the French connection cases. In 1979 the DEA rediscovered one of these chemists, André Bosquet, and alerted the Palermo police when he headed for Sicily. Bosquet kept giving the police the slip until they put three undercover men into his hotel, posing as staff members. Finally he was followed to his laboratory, a half-finished villa down a dusty road among orchards near Palmero. The villa, it turned out, was owned by the sister-in-law of Gerlando Alberti, a famous mafioso. Twenty police surrounded the villa before anyone had a chance to escape and arrested both Bosquet and Alberti. The next day they raided yet another villa, which also turned out to be a laboratory. There they found equipment that in a week could produce 50 kilos of heroin—worth $150 million in the United States—as well as a BMW, stolen in Milan, that had been fitted with hidden containers.

Alberti was jailed, but apparently not quite finished. One of the police who raided the villa was recognized as having been at Bosquet's hotel, where he had been an undercover agent. Three days later, two young men showed up at the hotel and asked to see the owner. When he arrived, they shot him in the face. Alberti, the police believed, had ordered the vengeance killing.

Since then other labs have been seized. A policeman on a routine patrol stumbled on an operating lab in Palermo; when the police closed in, they found 40 kilos of heroin, 50 kilos of morphine base, and equipment able to produce 100 kilos of heroin a week. But the refining is by no means limited to Sicily and the Sicilian Mafia. Corsicans have been smuggling morphine through Italy to the French-Italian border area, where French chemists, as in the old French connection days, have been refining it into heroin. DEA officials and Italian police have broken up a number of these labs, but it is clear that they are growing in number as fast as they can be destroyed. And the drug traffickers seem to have no trouble buying and smuggling in enough morphine to keep their equipment running.

Most of the heroin that leaves these laboratories is taken by car to an Italian international airport—usually Rome, sometimes Palermo. Couriers then carry the drug aboard in a hidden compartment of a suitcase or on their own body, usually in one- or two-kilo amounts. Heroin is also sent from such seaports as Palermo and Marseille. New York customs officials found 21 kilos in a container-load of furniture sent by boat from Palermo. At the other end of these shipments, no matter how they arrive, is the American side of the crime syndicate. Corsicans deal with Corsican Americans who have long traded in heroin, and the Sicilian Mafia deals with its own overseas branch—the American division of the Sicilian families. Once heroin reaches these people—after beginning months before as a pod waving in a Pakistani or Afghan field; crossing the vast, empty plains of Central Asia; being driven through the noisy, riotous bazaars of Turkey; rolling over hundreds of miles of river and mountain

A multi-kilo seizure of heroin. (DRUG ENFORCEMENT ADMINISTRATION)

and meadow in southern and eastern Europe; and finally arriving in Italy in the hands of the Cosa Nostra or a Corsican gang—it is only days away from the junkies of New York or Washington or Chicago, who will lay down $10 or $20 for a few hours of blessed numbness.

COCAINE

THE SMUGGLING of cocaine works in the opposite way from the smuggling of Golden Crescent heroin. The heroin passes from Pathans to Kurds to Turkish guest workers to Sicilian or Corsican mobsters to American crime families. Most cocaine begins and ends with Colombian families. Often a single group buys the coca, transports it, refines it into cocaine, hires couriers to bring it into the United States, sells it to wholesalers, and arranges the American bank accounts that make it possible to conceal the vast profits. Most narcotics agents believe that the Mafia has also gotten involved with cocaine—the Mafia does not usually pass up opportunities to make large profits in illegal business—by regularly buying the drug from Colombian outfits and selling it to wholesalers. And the growing population of Cubans in Miami and New York has increasingly made its way into the cocaine business, though usually at the bottom, as dealers. Both the Mafia and the Colombians are organized in the form of families and, within the group, adhere to the family virtues of honor and obedience: you don't cheat your colleagues; you keep your place in the organization. Cubans, however, have no traditional crime organization; they work alone. For this reason the Sicilians and the Colombians feel that they can work with one another, but not, in a big way, with the Cubans.

Narcotics agents and journalists now speak of the Colombian Mafia, but no high-powered crime syndicate existed until Americans developed a taste for cocaine in the late 1960s. The actual origins of Colombian organized crime are probably earlier, since the Sicilians and Corsicans who controlled the old heroin trade began using South America, as well as Cuba, as a stop-off point for the heroin traffic after World War II. At this point the Lucky Luciano of the South American connection stepped in. His name was Auguste Ricorde, and he arrived in Argentina after the war. In Paris he had begun as a petty crook, a thug, and during the war he served as a Nazi informant. When France was liberated in 1945, he fled to South America rather than face prison or execution. There he went back to his old business, dabbling in prostitution and narcotics. The field was still wide open, since heroin had only recently been arriving in South America. Ricorde's great achievement was convincing pilots who had flown down from the United States to fly back with illegal goods, above all heroin and cocaine. There they could sell the drugs to members of organized crime. This remained a fairly small business until cocaine became popular in the United States. But Ricorde had established the pathways. When cocaine began to be shipped in bulk, it would be sent either by private or commercial plane.

In order to see how cocaine is smuggled out of Colom-

Auguste Ricorde, the ex-Nazi informant who developed the South American connection for cocaine as well as heroin. (DRUG ENFORCEMENT ADMINISTRATION)

bia and into the United States, we can look at the activities of one Colombian family, that of Libia Cardona, "the cocaine queen." Her career was detailed in *New Florida* magazine. Libia was around when the cocaine business was just developing. In the mid-1960s two Latin Americans, Alberto Bravo and Griselda Blanco, had taken up where Ricorde left off, creating a new cocaine network. Bravo and Blanco purchased coca leaves, made them into paste, refined them in laboratories in Bogotá and Medellín, and sent couriers by plane to America's large cities. Cocaine, like heroin, is carried into the United States mostly in very small amounts in the suitcases or on the bodies of couriers, or "mules." As Bravo and Blanco's operation expanded, their need for mules grew. Compared with the money available at the top of the cocaine business, the pay for mules was very low. But to the average Colombian, earning only a few hundred dollars a year, the thought of earning a year's salary just by flying back and forth from Bogotá to the United States is understandably tempting. And one of the poor boys who decided to leave the slums of Medellín for the high-rolling world of crime was Jaime, Libia's older brother.

Having established himself as a courier in the gang run

by Bravo and Blanco, Jaime invited a friend named Luis Gaviria, a peasant on a dairy farm, to join him. Gaviria had the right kind of experience—a long police record for robbery. Jaime introduced his new co-worker to his sister Libia, and soon the two were lovers. Luis and Libia began, like Jaime, as couriers, ferrying cocaine into the United States on international flights. Soon they had learned all the ins and outs of the trade, and when, in 1971, Bravo and Blanco offered their mules a chance to invest in the business, they jumped at it. Luis and Libia had gotten into the cocaine trade just as it was taking off.

Luis and Libia's profits got bigger and bigger, until they were able to form a smuggling operation of their own, and there was so much money to be made that Bravo and Blanco didn't challenge them. Like other Colombian smuggling gangs, this one consisted almost entirely of family. Any weak link could betray the whole gang. If everyone was family, everyone could be trusted. Soon Luis and Libia had their sisters and brothers, cousins and aunts and uncles and in-laws working for them as couriers, bodyguards, chauffeurs, and aides. Both of them set their mothers up in homes that they then used as *caletas*, or safe houses, where drugs, money, and guns could be kept. By the late 1970s Luis and Libia employed 150 people in Latin America and the United States, and almost all of them were relatives. By that time the organization was earning about $60 million a year in cocaine.

Luis and Libia now had the whole network: people to buy coca from the farmers, to transport it to Medellín and Bogotá, an expert cocaine chemist, safe houses in which to conduct their business, and couriers to carry the

cocaine to the United States. They still needed some way
of smuggling it past American customs inspectors at the
airport where the couriers would land. Luis's brother-in-
law, Ramiro Penagos, had a friend who owned a luggage
factory in Bogotá. When cocaine arrived at the safe
house, Ramiro would notify his friend, who would then
go to work at night with a few trusted employees. They
would remove the padding that lined the suitcase, stuff it
with cocaine, and put the bottom back in place. Only by
drilling into the suitcase could anyone detect the cocaine.
Ramiro's friend charged $400 for the work on each suit-
case.

Finally, the couriers needed identities. None of them
had passports or visas, after all, and they weren't about
to register their names in order to receive them. It was
important for the couriers to appear to be American citizens, since Colombians were much more likely to be
searched and questioned. Moreover, they had to keep
changing identities all the time to throw the American
authorities off balance. If they flew from Colombia to
Guatemala to the United States, they would have to enter
Guatemala with one false identity and enter the United
States with another. By now the main cities of Colombia
are teeming with men who will turn out false passports
and identity papers for a fee; it is an ancient art and
appears wherever smuggling is a way of life. Libia turned
to a forger in Bogotá whose nickname was Picasso; one
of the masters of his craft, Picasso then charged up to
$1,500 for a passport and has since raised his rates to
$3,000. With as many as forty or fifty mules making the
trip to the United States at any one time, this was an
expense of hundreds of thousands of dollars annually. A

passport, after all, is only the beginning. One mule arrested in Miami was found with a passport, a Florida driver's license, a Social Security card, a hospitalization card, and an alien resident card—all forged.

Probably nobody needs as many cards as that to prove his or her identity, but in the smuggling business, as in other forms of crime, nothing can be left to chance. And smugglers like Luis and Libia had so much money that they could go to incredible lengths to ensure that their couriers were not discovered. Flying from Bogotá directly to the United States, for example, seemed dangerous to them, because anybody coming off such a flight is more likely to be searched than someone arriving from a different country. The fact is that so many Colombians pass through American airports every year—half a million in Miami alone—that only a fraction of them can be searched, but Luis and Libia's fears were well grounded. They would send the courier to some intermediate place such as Panama, Guatemala, or the Bahamas on their way to Miami or Houston. At these in-between stops they would change airlines, clothes, and identities.

Once safely past American customs authorities, the courier could then proceed to one of the *caletas* that Luis and Libia had established in Miami and New York. These, too, were run by family members. Only when a high-level dealer came to the house to buy the cocaine for distribution did control over the drug finally leave the family. Luis and Libia, in other words, made their money from selling cocaine, which they bought in the form of coca paste, to wholesalers, not from selling it to users themselves. The big money is in smuggling and high-level

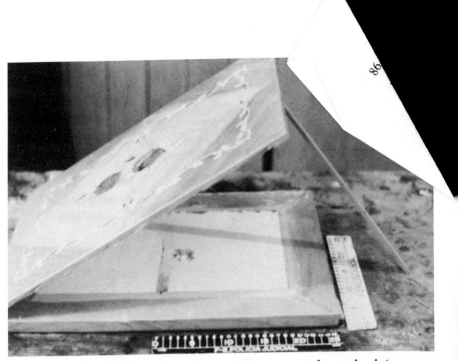

A framed painting used, unsuccessfully, to smuggle cocaine into the United States. (DRUG ENFORCEMENT ADMINISTRATION)

wholesaling. Libia and Luis bought their paste for $2,500 a kilo, spent another $12,500 a kilo getting it to the United States, and sold it for $60,000. And every month Luis and Libia were selling 90 or more kilos, earning $4 million in cash.

The same suitcases that left Bogotá lined with co-caine left the United States stuffed with money. After a big deal in Los Angeles Luis's sister-in-law returned to Bogotá with a color television set—an ordinary purchase for a South American visiting the United States. When Libia's chauffeur met the woman at the airport and drove her to Libia's fancy Bogotá home, she handed over the set, and the cocaine queen pried off the back and reoved $750,000 in $50 and $100 bills. She then counted out $300,000 for the sister-in-law and her husband, deposited $350,000 in her own Bogotá bank account, and invested $100,000 in Colombian coffee stock.

Libia and Luis lived like royalty. They kept apartments in New York City and apartments and homes in Miami. They bought several more apartments in Bogotá as well as a house in one of the city's wealthiest neighborhoods, all of which they redecorated with such ornaments as 24-karat gold bathroom fixtures. They bought a chicken farm two hours south of Bogotá and converted it into a huge laboratory and then destroyed the old farmhouse in order to build a multimillion dollar country estate with a ballroom, crystal chandeliers, Italian marble tile, a swimming pool, and a sauna. They also bought their own airline, Opita, which had five passenger planes flying around Colombia, and a private jet in which Luis and Libia could follow their smuggling activities. Opita's headquarters were three floors below the office of the DEA.

Sudden wealth does not usually satisfy greed, it only encourages it all the more; and greed eventually destroyed the Cardona-Gaviria empire, as it does many others. In May 1977 Libia's sister Luz and another courier, Grettal William Ramirez, were arrested in Houston. Libia sent Luis's niece to Houston with bail money for Luz and word for Ramirez that if he kept his mouth shut and went to jail, he would be freed quickly and paid well and that if he cooperated with the police, he would be killed.

Couriers are made to understand from the very beginning that they must protect the secrecy of the organiza-

tion on pain of death. A single weak lin.
tioned earlier, can bring down the whole c
Libia's offer to Ramirez was not an unusual on.
had every reason to believe that her threat was rea.
mule arrested in Miami, not connected to the Cardon.
gang, told police, "They told me that my entire family—
and myself—would be killed if I betrayed them. And I
believe it. Seven men and three women in one family of
my acquaintance were killed by machine gun fire when
the courier betrayed the organization." The police convinced this man to work as an undercover agent for
them—to pretend that he had not been arrested, to continue to work with his superiors, and thus eventually to
lead the police to them—in exchange for his freedom.
"He's playing a very dangerous game," said one of the
narcotics agents involved with the scheme. "If the organization ever suspected he had turned informant, his
life wouldn't be worth a peso. But that's the way the
game is played."

Libia's mistake was her failure to take care of Ramirez
as she had promised. But Luis made a more serious error. The mobsters with whom he was arranging an enormous 400-kilo sale accused him of cutting the purity of
part of the shipment. Luis first denied it, and then admitted it. That night he went out, and when he returned to
the lobby of the Queens apartment that he shared with
Libia, a shot rang out, and Luis toppled forward in a pool
of blood. Detectives interrogated Libia, but she told
them nothing and fled the next day back to Bogotá. There
she took total control of the organization by removing all
of Luis's relatives, even evicting Luis's mother from the
caleta. Meanwhile, though, Ramirez had not been re-

warded for his silence, and he struck back from jail. Back in Bogotá, Luz was murdered by gunfire while walking to Libia's home.

Most people, after the murder of their husband and sister, would have given up cocaine and retired to their mansions and apartments. Libia Cardona was not, however, a person of ordinary willpower. She continued to operate her cocaine business from a discreet distance, and she finally paid the price. Another mule who she neglected agreed to help the police, and in December 1980 Libia, another sister, and a cousin were arrested in Miami. Bail was set at $5 million. Her lawyer pleaded that she could not make even $1 million in bail. The judge lowered bail to $3 million. The lawyer pleaded again. The judge lowered bail again to $1 million and allowed her actually to post much less. This time she posted bail, as did her sister and cousin. For one month she reported daily to her probation officer. Then, having established her apparently honest intentions, Libia, her sister, and her cousin escaped to the Bahamas, and from there back to their mansions in Bogotá. This set of events, as we will see later on, is par for the course.

The cocaine smuggling business is not run entirely by Colombian gangs. Some-free lancers, mostly Americans, work alone, but they are probably a vanishing species. Most of them began by smuggling marijuana and then moved on to cocaine when they realized how much more profitable it was and how much easier to handle. Towns like Tingo Maria and Cochabamba, in Bolivia, as well as Bogotá and Medellín, are aswarm with small smugglers from South America as well as the United

States. These people do not have enormous organi, tions and immense quantities of money to spend on every possible precaution, and they have to make up for it with ingenuity.

One of the cleverest of these smugglers was Zachary Swan, a businessman from New York, and the subject of a book called *Snow Blind,* by Robert Sabbag. Rather than dispatch couriers on planes, as a large organization would, Swan sent cocaine through the mail, usually to post office boxes he had rented. Owing to the possibility of the package being opened, Swan tried to send his cocaine in the most innocent-looking objects. He noticed that tourists in Bogotá often bought rolling pins made of a native wood, so he decided to store the drug in homemade versions of them. He had a carpenter in Bogotá carve rolling pins identical to the ones sold in tourist shops, except that he would cut them in half down the middle. Then the carpenter would hollow out either side, line the inside with plastic, and fill it with cocaine. Then he would close it with glue and clamps, paint and finish it so that the slice was invisible. Inside one pin Swan could pack as many as 3 kilos of coke, because he had bought an ancient press with which he and two accomplices squeezed the cocaine into tiny blocks. Once the rolling pin was packaged, Swan and his two accomplices would address it. For fear that their handwriting might be recognized, each would write every third letter.

Swan became very wealthy in the cocaine business, though his income was nothing compared with that of a major Colombian trafficker. It was not so much, in any case, that he had trouble spending it fairly quickly. One problem he had, though, was where to hide his money. In Colombia nobody asks questions when you deposit $300,000 in a bank, at least if you know the right bank. The same, as we shall see later on, is often true in the United States, but it is a far riskier proposition.

Since Swan lived most of the time in New York and preferred not to use a bank, he hid his money in a way that perfectly paralleled the way he earned it—inside logs. With his usual fanatical attention to the important details, Swan floated logs in his bathtub for two or three days until the bark came off. Then he cut a hole in the wood exactly the same size as the currency he had to conceal, and stuffed in the money. Finally he replaced the bark with glue, clamps, and rope. And he lived in fear that one of his houseguests would try to start a fire with the wrong log.

Zachary Swan was also eventually arrested, and he, too, spent only a short time in jail before gaining his freedom. That, as we shall see, is the way it usually is with drug smugglers.

MARIJUANA

More than cocaine or certainly heroin, marijuana smuggling is the crime of the independent operator, the man or woman who enjoys using the drug, likes the adventure of smuggling it, and talks of settling down after one last, especially big haul to a peaceful, law-abiding life. Many of them, however, get arrested, or even killed, just before arriving at that promised land. The smugglers seem to have all the advantages over the police, but sooner or later somebody makes a mistake—out of greed, more often than mere carelessness—and the high rollers pay the price.

Until the marijuana crop was cut down in Mexico and relocated in Colombia, smuggling was almost entirely a game of the inspired amateur. In the 1960s pot smoking had an air of social and political protest: I'll get stoned while my parents and their friends insist on their boring sobriety; I'll break the law while everyone else obeys foolish and hypocritical laws. Smuggling had much the same appeal. Many of the smugglers were hippies who drifted down to Mexico, smoked pot, barely knew what they were doing, and often got caught. Buying marijuana was no trouble at all. You had only to buy a used car, drive down to Culiacán, in Durango, and then bluff your way past the American border guards on the way back. If you made it with your 50 to 100 pounds, you weren't going to be rich, but you could live well, and smoke well, for a while. A Robin Hood air of harmless piracy marked the whole business, and it seemed a far cry from the brutality and destructivenesss of the heroin trade. The marijuana smugglers may have been outlaws, in their own mind, but they were not criminals.

As the Border Patrol began to figure out the smuggling business, anyone who looked like a smuggler, drove a typical smuggler's car, or used typical smuggler's hiding places was in trouble. Enforcement, as usual, created clever dodges instead of wiping out the business. Zachary Swan, once again, offers an impressive example of strategy. Swan first got into the drug business in the ordi-

Marijuana packed into a one kilo brick for shipment. (DRUG ENFORCEMENT ADMINISTRATION)

nary way, driving down to Mexico, sitting around until the marijuana he had ordered was delivered, hiring a mule to drive it over the border, and then returning to the United States to pick up the load.

This method quickly became too time-consuming and dangerous, so Swan started thinking up better ones. He bought a pickup truck for $3,500, and placed a classified ad in the *Village Voice*, a New York newspaper, offering "Camper for rent; ideal for Mexico." Swan waited weeks until he received the perfect request—from a pair of Long Island high school teachers who wanted a summer vacation. Swan not only suggested they drive to Mexico, but gave them the name of a friend who would put them up for free in a villa in Acapulco. The friend was Swan's drug contact. Sure enough, the two teachers headed straight for Acapulco and moved into the friend's villa. They had a lovely stay, save that their camper, oddly enough, developed an oil leak. A man who worked at the villa offered to fix it. The man was "Nice Mickey," another accomplice. Mickey caused the oil leak in the first place, and when he returned the camper he had added 200 pounds of marijuana to its underside. The teachers, completely ignorant of the scheme, drove the camper back to New York and delivered to Swan a cargo of marijuana worth $12,000. A gentle sort, Swan made sure that his unknowing helpers would escape trouble in case they were caught. He made sure that they carried with them the ad he had written, so they could prove that they were innocent victims. And Swan protected himself by offering the van from an apartment that he had rented under an assumed name.

Independent smugglers like Swan are still engaged in a daily battle of wits with the Border Patrol, but the scene has largely shifted to Colombia. Moving marijuana from Colombia to the United States is obviously a much more complex enterprise than smuggling it from Mexico. Now the trafficker has two borders, as well as several hundred, or thousand, miles of water to cross. This is a job for professionals and professional organizations. Not all of these organizations are Colombian, however. The Colombians have made cocaine, which is more profitable and much neater, their own business, leaving part of the marijuana trade to the Americans and Cubans.

Colombians control all marijuana smuggling up to the water's edge. Despite enforcement efforts by the Colombian police, almost all marijuana leaves Colombia from the province of La Guajira, whose coast has been controlled by smugglers since the arrival of the Spanish in 1520. Whether the drug is to be put aboard a boat or a plane, it will be loaded by Guajiros, and many of them serve on the boats themselves. The Guajiros have earned a cutthroat reputation similar to that of most coastal pirates. These professional smugglers, writes Hank Messick, author of *Of Grass and Snow*, "have dedicated themselves to illegal business such as contraband. And they use, above everything else, revenge. They do not trust justice, only the gun."

No one person established the Colombian marijuana trade as Alberto Bravo and Griselda Blanco, or Auguste Ricorde, did with the cocaine trade. But the basic smuggling method was developed by two American businessmen named John Steele and Herbert Denber. In the early 1970s Denber and Steele began running a 110-foot freighter, the *Night Train*, back and forth between La Guajira and southern Florida, carrying tons of marijuana. The *Night Train* became a legend among smugglers as well as frustrated narcotics agents, and its successful technique was soon imitated.

The method that Denber and Steele invented, and that now reigns in the marijuana business, moves in several stages. It begins with one of the principals of the smuggling ring flying to Colombia to arrange the purchase of as much marijuana as can be stuffed into a large freighter or shrimp boat—as much as 20 tons. Then the boat, known as a mother ship, is brought into one of La Guajira's innumerable harbors, loaded with as much as 300,000 dollars' worth of marijuana, and sent off toward

Tons of marijuana confiscated by the police. (DRUG ENFORCEMENT ADMINISTRATION)

southern Florida, with its own innumerable harbors and 3,000 miles of coastline.

Meanwhile, in southern Florida, another member of the gang is making a different set of arrangements. First this member finds a crew to unload the bales of marijuana into a truck when it arrives. This is exhausting work, but it pays $5,000 to $10,000 for a single night—an incredible amount of money for a few hours of work, but insignificant to the smugglers. Anyone who hangs around dockside bars for a few days has no trouble finding volunteers for the unloading work. Then the gang member has to scout the coastline to find a secluded cove or inlet, or even a pier, where marijuana can be unloaded and thrown immediately into the backs of waiting trucks. Southern Florida does not lack for such places.

Finally, this gang member must find a pilot for the

group's speedboat. The cigarette boat—as it is also called, because such boats were used in tobacco smuggling in the 1930s—is the crucial innovation in the mother ship system. The mother ship itself, laden with 40,000 pounds of marijuana, would be a sitting duck for the police as it approached land. As long as it remains more than 12 miles off the coast, however, it is safe. The United States, like all countries that border on the sea, has territorial waters that extend for 12 miles; beyond this limit it cannot enforce its laws. So the mother ship hovers as much as 50 miles offshore, out of reach of the police. The purpose of the cigarette boats is to ferry the marijuana, in small bundles and at terrific speed, to shore. An expert pilot can demand $50,000 for a single night's work. Many of the boats can do 70 miles an hour and are equipped with radar scanners and infrared night-vision scopes. Fully equipped, they cost $250,000. And as often as not they're abandoned after a single use. The boat could be recognized, and the quarter of a million dollars means little to a ring importing 15 million dollars' worth of marijuana.

In the cat-and-mouse game that they play with enforcement agents, smugglers have found that a rusty old shrimp boat hovering in international waters for a few days attracts increasing attention from Coast Guard cutters on the prowl. Many of them have thus begun using the Bahamas as an unloading station. At their westernmost edge the Bahamas are only 60 miles from the Florida coast, easily within range of a cigarette boat or a light aircraft. And the relaxed atmosphere of this resort nation has made smuggling easy work. Local citizens can

A Columbian trawler (bow furthest left) surrounded by police and Coast Guard boats after the trawler, a drug mother ship was seized off Long Island with seventeen tons of marijuana on board. (WIDE WORLD PHOTOS)

A Coast Guard vessel crammed with tons of marijuana from a mother ship. (DRUG ENFORCEMENT ADMINISTRATION)

easily be recruited to provide aid. Many of the smugglers who use the Bahamas fly their marijuana from Colombia in private planes. A Bahamian who lights up a rough airstrip in the forest, or merely provides gasoline, can earn $10,000 in an evening. The rates for unloading a mother ship are equally high.

Since the late 1970s the Bahamas have become a second home for marijuana smugglers, and the country threatens to become as wide open and corrupt as Cuba was in the 1940s or 1950s, when the Mafia used it as a jumping-off point for heroin (though the Bahamian government, unlike the Cuban government of that time, deplores the rise in crime). A crime wave has terrorized the waters around the islands, to the point where many pleasure boaters have decided to remain on land. Two Americans in a 40-foot boat, for example, were attacked by armed men in four speedboats. The men were demanding drugs, and when the Americans said they had none, the smugglers opened fire, eventually sinking the boat's dinghy. Incidents like this have become common.

The smugglers have also begun to steer clear of southern Florida when possible, since drug enforcement efforts have been concentrated there. Almost every major port along the southeast coast has reported marijuana seizures. Georgia has much the same kind of coastline as southern Florida, wrinkled with tiny inlets, and has become the second most popular state for smugglers. And as the pressure mounts they move farther north, to South Carolina and even as far as Tennessee. In March 1981 the Nashville police seized 640 pounds of cocaine from a twin-engine jet that had landed in a local airport. The street value of the cocaine was estimated at $240 million—the second largest coke bust ever.

And as they move northward, smugglers also move westward, across the Gulf of Mexico. The swampy bayous of Louisiana have always sheltered smugglers, and some of them now drift quietly through the marshes in barges laden with as much as 80 tons of marijuana. Since 1976 Texas has become a major port for smugglers, and home to some major smuggling rings. One group brought in 172,000 pounds of marijuana in five trips from Colombia before they were caught. This smooth operation was funded by a multimillionaire retired businessman and seemed to be connected, although nothing was ever proven, to a major force in Texas politics and business, Rex Cauble. The group swiftly brought their tonnage from the coast to one of Cauble's several ranches. At one of the ranches buyers from all over the country would park their vans and campers by a nearby riverbank and wait while one of Cauble's ranch hands took their vehicles and returned them loaded with the requested amount of marijuana. Four years after they started, this gang was broken up. The small fry were arrested when one of them failed to pay off a boat captain, who then alerted the DEA. And some of the bigger fish were caught when one of the small fry got tired of waiting for the money for bail and lawyers, which he had been told to expect if he ever wound up in jail. The same weaknesses seem to reappear in every drug smuggling ring, no matter what the drug.

Not only can smugglers move all along the southeastern and southwestern coasts to escape detection, they can also avoid the coastline altogether by packing their marijuana into a plane and landing at a remote airstrip not an airport, of course, but merely a clearing in the jungle or the woods. La Guajira province is marked with tiny scars in the forest where experienced pilots can touch down with such ancient planes as DC-4s. From there they can fly to the Bahamas and transfer their stash to a lighter plane that can land even more easily and more readily escape detection in the United States. Or they can fly directly to one of southern Florida's 250 airstrips or somewhere else farther north or west.

An experienced pilot can expect to clear as much as $100,000 for a single trip, but the work is hazardous: the planes often crash while trying to land, perhaps because the fumes from the tons of marijuana affect the pilot. Another tactic, highly dangerous, is to swoop low over the ground and drop bales of marijuana at a prearranged spot. Sometimes this is done in the middle of the Gulf of

Mexico, with speedboats waiting nearby. Another favorite spot is at the Opa-Locka airport, literally next door to DEA headquarters in Miami. The planes fly low just beneath commercial flights, so that the radar won't pick them up, and drop cocaine and marijuana to accomplices waiting below. The planes, like the equally expensive cigarette boats, aren't expected to last long; at the slightest sign of danger they are abandoned. A new one can always be bought, or stolen. In 1980 alone, 241 private planes were stolen, two-thirds of them, it is estimated, by drug rings.

With so much money and so many options, American marijuana rings are often as complex and careful as Colombian families like the Cardona-Gaviria group we mentioned earlier. Many of them, however, are a good deal more peaceable, and perhaps would never engage in business that they thought was illegitimate rather than merely illegal.

Donald Steinberg, for example, was a young pot smoker in the late 1960s who began selling to pay for his own use. His business got bigger and bigger until, first, it became a full-time profession and, then, an immense enterprise. By 1978 he and his friends were importing 500,000 pounds of marijuana every year and earning $100 million. They needed a special plane to take their piles of cash to cooperative banks outside the United States. Steinberg lived in a $400,000 house in Fort Lauderdale and kept a $2 million town house in New York City. He and his crew learned the ins and outs of international finance and kept an untraceable flow of money moving from bank to bank all over the world. They started their own marijuana business in Kenya. Steinberg probably had one of the world's richest marijuana businesses but, he says, "I never saw a gun the whole time I was in the business." He and his group had standing rules against the use of force. But they ended the way most others do. Quite by accident the police caught on, and after more than a year they finally arrested him: he had given his home phone number to his veterinarian out of fear for the health of his Saint Bernard.

Marijuana smuggling, despite the high risk and sometimes deadly consequences (for example, Herbert Denber, the father of the mother ship, was murdered in 1976, apparently by Cubans whom he had double-crossed) still appeals to the happy-go-lucky in people. One of the crewmen on the *Agnes Pauline,* a shrimp boat run by the big Texas gang mentioned earlier, was Les Fuller, who had made a quiet living running Cutter Bill's Western World, a chain of stores owned by Rex Cauble. But Fuller apparently always wanted to be a cowboy; he came to his office daily in a big white cowboy hat, tall, ornate boots with his jeans tucked in, and a pinkie ring of pure gold shaped like the state of Texas. Smuggling was as close to the cowboy life as he could get. Another crew member, James Longendyke, also an amateur, was asked by a narcotics official why he got involved with smugglers. He answered, "Sailin' to Colombia with a bunch of naked women. Sneakin' past the Coast Guard. Hell, that's Erroll Flynn stuff. I'd've done it for free."

The police and federal agents in southern Florida seize 3.2 million pounds of marijuana each year, though this amounts to only 15 percent or so of the quantity that Americans smoke. At one point the police were holding so much marijuana that, instead of merely burning it, they took it to the Florida Power and Light Company, where they discovered that 732 pounds of marijuana creates as much electricity as one barrel of oil. The Customs Service in Florida also had, as of 1981, two hundred cigarette boats and fifty airplanes, including an A-26 bomber from the World War II era that Customs had used in drug cases before it was bought by smugglers.

Enforcement agents have a wide variety of ways of capturing marijuana smugglers, some of which we will discuss in the next section. What is essential in all enforcement efforts is to gain the confidence of the smugglers. Often this is done by arresting, or threatening to arrest, members of a gang and then offering to keep them out of jail if they work as undercover agents. Southern Florida is a beehive of local, state, and federal

Marijuana being unloaded on to shore—the off-loaders may make $10,000 each. (DRUG ENFORCEMENT ADMINISTRATION)

police, their undercover agents and informers, smugglers, and smugglers who are also agents—or were, or seem to be—all spying on one another. It is a confusing and highly dangerous way of breaking smuggling rings, but, as we will see in our discussion of heroin dealers in New York, it works.

A special police tactic in trying to arrest groups who smuggle marijuana by mother ship is to pose as someone in the business of aiding the smugglers. In a major DEA case, Operation Grouper, federal agents posed as off-loaders, working the Texas coast. To protect their scheme, the agents would complete the job, and the smugglers would be arrested only later on. And they did a good job. "We became so popular we had to turn business away," one of the agents said later. In twenty-two months Operation Grouper seized a billion dollars' worth of drugs, thirty mother ships, two airplanes, a million dollars in cash, and 155 suspected smugglers. In a similar case in Texas a DEA agent posed as a marina manager, permitting himself to be bribed so that smugglers could unload right on his dock. His biggest catch was the gang operating a ship called the *Mister Jake*, which pulled into the marina carrying 50 tons of marijuana. The moment the first 60-pound bale was unloaded, the federal agents moved in.

One of the most famous and daring Operation Grouper cases was the interception, at long last, of the gang operating the notorious *Night Train*. One of the smugglers approached the agents, who were posing as off-loaders, with the fabulous offer of 10 percent of a $12 million cargo if they would run a launch out to the ship, take the marijuana to a loading area, and place it in waiting trucks. The arrangements became immensely complicated as the smugglers became nervous, and the agents were forced to wait for days before finally receiving the go-ahead. Finally they pushed off into the Gulf south of Florida and waited, again, until a plane circled overhead and dropped a series of notes in bottles providing directions to the mother ship. Until then the smugglers had refused to reveal the location. As soon as they had the information the agents notified another team of agents who were hiding in a nearby lagoon in a Coast Guard cutter. The cutter immediately raced out to the indicated area, and the agents were startled and thrilled to find that it was the famous *Night Train*. When the crew realized that they had been double-crossed, they tried to ram and sink the cutter. The swifter boat got by them, however, and fired a cannon shot across the *Night Train's* bow as a sign of seriousness. At this point the crew, largely Guajiro, surrendered, and the *Night Train* was retired to history.

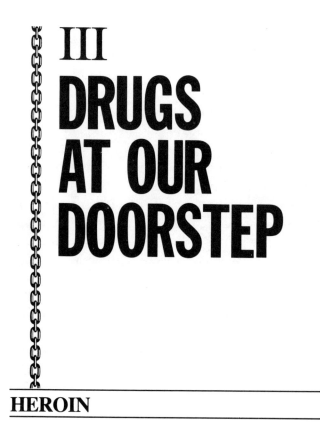

III
DRUGS AT OUR DOORSTEP

HEROIN

NEW YORK has the dubious distinction of being the nation's heroin capital. Heroin from Southwest Asia arrives directly on international flights into Kennedy Airport, in the luggage or on the person of a courier. Southeast Asian heroin, coming from the other side of the world, often enters North America from the West Coast, in Los Angeles or Vancouver, but eventually finds its way to a buyer from New York. And Mexican heroin supplies much of the West and the Midwest, but a large fraction of it is also driven over the border and on to New York.

For many years heroin distribution lay almost completely in the hands of the Mafia and the Corsicans. Most heroin came along the route stretching between Turkey and southern France, a trade, as we have seen, that is dominated by Sicilians and Corsicans. Most of these crime families had branches in the United States. The heroin that was dropped off by the European branch was picked up by the American branch and whomever that family worked with. The Corsicans, for instance, worked with Cubans who lived in New Jersey and Miami. The Sicilian Mafia also worked with blacks.

The breaking of the French connection and the arrival of heroin from other parts of the world brought new groups to power, though organized crime has never lost its ability to call the shots. First, the Cubans, who had bought all of their heroin through France, left the heroin business (they turned, as we shall see later, to cocaine). The Corsicans also largely lost out. When heroin began arriving from the Golden Triangle in the early 1970s, the Chinese suddenly became prominent in the heroin world. As we mentioned earlier, they work largely through other Chinese, which meant that immense sums of money were suddenly up for grabs in Chinese communities in America's big cities. More than one Chinatown was rocked by "tong wars," deadly battles for turf between rival gangs. From 1971 to 1972 San Francisco was the scene of savage youth wars, in which gangs under the protection of different Triads began destroying one another and even rebelling against their elders—an unheard-of event in Chinese society. During that year at least thirty people were murdered by one side or another. A young man named Raymond Leung announced that he would join a friend's crusade to end the fighting. The next day a gunman walked up to him in broad daylight and shot him at practically point-blank range with a .38. Leung staggered forward while literally hundreds of passersby watched, and one of three gunmen stood directly over him and fired a .45 into his head. It is a special mark of drug wars that they are more often than not civil wars, pitting Colombians, blacks, or Chinese against one another.

But the Chinese never dominated the selling process even of Southeast Asian heroin. They needed someone who knew the customers and the city, who could move inconspicuously on the street, who knew which cops to bribe and which to avoid. In New York the Chinese worked largely with Hispanics, while Sicilians often used blacks to sell heroin on the street. Many of the addicts, after all, were poor blacks and Hispanics who lived in the ghetto, so it seemed logical, though also painfully ironic, that their own people should sell to them. During the 1960s black dealers, especially, got closer and closer to the heroin source, challenging the Mafia for control. A number of black wholesalers even began providing their own supply by going directly to France or Italy to buy heroin, thus bypassing the Italians who normally sold to them.

The first black trafficker to stand up to the mob was Frank Matthews, who in the mid-1960s began buying his heroin from Cubans and French Corsicans. Within a few years Matthews was selling his own brand of heroin through candy stores all over Harlem. Soon he expanded his business up and down the East Coast and then moved on to Cleveland, Chicago, Detroit, Cincinnati, and elsewhere. Certain parts of each of those cities were understood to be his and his alone. One evening he decided to impress a friend by taking him along as he made collections of heroin money from New York on down to Philadelphia. He collected his cash in bags, and by the time he left New York he had to throw out his spare tire to make room for the money. By the time he finished, he had torn out the whole back seat to make space available. When he drove home, he opened up a closet to reveal stacks of cash six feet high. No non-Italian or non-Corsican had ever been this high up on the heroin totem pole; Matthews had hundreds of people working for him. In four years he cleared $100 million. And he got away with it. In 1973 he disappeared with a girl friend, a bodyguard, and $20 million. He has never been seen since.

The gaudy world of heroin dealers is not so different from that of the opium warlords in Southeast Asia. Each controls his own piece of turf, and he will kill anyone inside that territory who steps out of line or anyone who tries to muscle in from the outside. And when a kingpin departs, someone else comes along to take his place. When Frank Matthews disappeared, his power and wealth were inherited by the infamous Leroy "Nicky" Barnes, who might be thought of as the Khun Sa of the Harlem heroin traffic. Like the Burmese warlord, Barnes built up his contacts carefully and soon came to control a vast stretch of territory; like Khun Sa, Barnes seemed utterly invulnerable to attack or arrest, eluding the police and destroying his enemies. Perhaps the major difference between the two lies in the fact that Khun Sa believes that he is fighting for a cause, while the only cause that Nicky Barnes had was himself. For us, though, he provides an opportunity to see how the drug business works on the streets, and to see what the police can do to stop it.

Nicky Barnes was born in Harlem, and by the time he was twelve or thirteen he was already addicted to heroin. Thousands of other boys like him get hooked all the time, begin stealing to support their habit, shuttle back and forth between the streets and the prisons or treatment clinics, and, more often than not, die young. Nicky Barnes, however, was strong-willed from the start. He shook off his addiction, took up weightlifting, and decided to make himself rich. And the quickest way to get rich in a ghetto like Harlem—the quickest way to get rich anywhere, for that matter—is through crime. And the most profitable crime going is drug trafficking. So Nicky Barnes decided to get in on the other side of the heroin business.

At first Barnes hustled heroin on the street, like other kids. But throughout the 1950s and early 60s he was assembling a Dominican connection, working with other Hispanics who were selling heroin at the street level. Barnes began buying heroin in larger amounts and selling it to pushers. Then in 1965 Barnes had his first big break. On one of his numerous, though always brief, visits to prison—he was arrested thirteen times between 1950 and 1977—Barnes met Joey Gallo, boss of the Gallo family, which controlled heroin in Harlem. Barnes had never been important enough to deal directly with the Mafia. He might buy, instead, from a so-called front-line dealer or wholesaler who bought from the Mafia, which actually controlled the heroin as it arrived by plane or boat. Now, however, Barnes had an Italian connection, and suddenly he was able to buy more and more heroin. His own network grew larger, and he moved further and further from street dealing.

Barnes was also more or less protected from the savage war taking place between blacks and Italians for control of the heroin trade. The dominance of organized crime in the drug business had never been challenged before, and during the late 1960s blood ran in the streets of Harlem. It was like the war between the Shan States Army and the KMT Army taking place at much the same time 10,000 miles away. But it was an uneven battle. Organized crime had more guns and more soldiers, and since then no one has challenged the Mafia's demand to be cut into the heroin business. Barnes, meanwhile, was buying his heroin through the Italians. And when the French connection was broken and his suppliers lost their source of heroin, Barnes hardly skipped a beat before moving heavily into Mexican heroin, which began arriving in bulk in the early 1970s. And by the mid-1970s, when Mexican heroin, known as brown sugar, was flooding the streets, and three-quarters of a million addicts were paying to support their habit, Nicky Barnes was a kingpin.

Barnes was, in fact, practically a legend. Kids in Harlem looked up to him as if he were a sports hero, an image that Barnes carefully groomed. He handed out turkeys in Harlem and gave lavish gifts. He lived like a king: he was said to own three hundred suits, a hundred pairs of shoes, fifty leather coats. Modesty was not part of his image, and sometimes he would interrupt a show in a club to announce that he, Nicky Barnes, had arrived. He was both a Robin Hood and a gigantic mobster. Everyone knew what he did, but the police seemed pow-

Heroin, ready for the streets. (DRUG ENFORCEMENT ADMINISTRATION)

erless to stop him, which only added to his appeal in Harlem. Seven times he was arrested, and each time, with the aid of high-priced lawyers and, at times, shoddy police work, he escaped scot-free. The blood, like the heroin, never showed up on Barnes's hands. When the police raided his apartment in 1973, they found a .25-caliber automatic pistol, a .32-caliber Smith and Wesson revolver, a .32-caliber Clerke revolver, and a .38-caliber handgun. But they couldn't prove that the apartment belonged to Barnes. He was charged with murdering a man with a penknife in 1974 and later acquitted. When his lieutenants, who actually sold the heroin, seemed to be holding back some of the profits, they didn't last long. One of them, Reggie Isaacs, was found murdered on the eighteenth hole of a golf course; another, Stanley Morgan, was found with eight bullet holes in him, next to a police station (a small touch that Barnes must have enjoyed). And there was more—fires, torture, bribes—but Barnes always emerged clean.

Barnes had a first-class operation going, buying from high-ranking Sicilians, selling high-quality, high-purity material. He had his own brand names: Dy-no-mite, Wow, Zap. He kept twenty to thirty apartments around New York simply to serve as "mills," where heroin was cut and bagged. The women who did this manual labor sat in long rows, naked; with their clothes on they could hide some of the heroin to sell or use themselves. Each pound or kilo was divided into small portions and then mixed with quinine or lactose or a number of other white, tasteless substances. Usually one part heroin would be combined with four to five parts mix. Then a few grams would be dropped into each of thousands of small plastic bags.

From the mill the bagged heroin was taken to another apartment or clubhouse or abandoned factory or garage, from which Barnes's organization would actually do the selling. Barnes himself never touched heroin, and only rarely personally accepted money, a fact that made it practically impossible to arrest him. The heroin was sold by Barnes's most trusted lieutenants to wholesalers who might buy as much as a pound or so and pay for their purchase with shopping bags full of cash. They in turn sold it to other middlemen, who sold it to pushers, who actually sold the nickel bags to junkies. By the mid-1970s Barnes's gang was earning at least a million dollars a month from heroin as well as some cocaine, and the organization controlled large portions of Harlem, New Jersey, and Long Island, and parts of the Midwest. And Barnes himself had become famous as "Mr. Untouchable," the man whom the police could not catch.

But Barnes eventually was caught, and the way it was done gives some insight into how very difficult it is to catch a drug trafficker as careful and powerful as he. From the late 1960s onward both the New York City police and federal agents knew that Barnes was a major violator, and they spared no effort to put him in jail. At one point he was even kept under twenty-four-hour surveillance for eight months, but the police never caught him selling drugs or committing any other felony.

Most big-time traffickers have become so careful about directly committing crimes that the police have turned more and more to conspiracy charges. That is, instead of arresting a trafficker for selling heroin, they arrest him or her for conspiring with others to do so. A conspiracy is much more difficult to prove than a simple crime. The police must show that an individual created an organization that does all the things that drug syndicates do and that this individual controls the organization. And the only way to do this is to get inside the organization by planting informants and secretly tape-recording conversations. Everything that the informant records as well as everything that he or she observes can then be pieced together at a trial to prove the conspiracy charge.

What the informant has to record, ultimately, is a drug transaction. It's not enough for the trafficker to say that his business is illegal narcotics; he or one of his lieutenants has to sell some, agree to sell some, or be in the room while narcotics are being sold. This means that the police have to be able to buy drugs, a very expensive proposition. One of the great problems in drug enforcement has been that police budgets have gone up much more slowly than the cost of drugs. The police simply don't have the money to buy the drugs to keep several investigations going at once. An initial investment of half an ounce may cost $5,000, though the same amount in a period when heroin was more plentiful and cheap, as in the mid-1970s, might have been only $2,500. But the police can't stop after a single small purchase. The "buy and bust" method that both local police and federal agents use requires that informants or undercover cops start at the bottom and buy their way to the top, stopping only when they feel that the investigation can go no higher.

To catch a significant dealer, an agent has to buy in amounts not less than one-eighth of a kilo, or about four ounces, and to do so more than once. The investigation of Nicky Barnes, for example, cost about $70,000 in drug money alone, though heroin was far cheaper then than it is now. Yet as of 1981 the entire New York City police force had only $700,000 in "buy money," down from $2.5 million in the French connection days of the early seventies. The DEA's northeast regional office had only $1 million in buy money. A task force on narcotics, which the regional office operates along with New York State and City police had an additional $500,000. The total of $2 million or so is so little that many investigations simply cannot be begun and others have to be abandoned because the undercover agents run out of money.

The investigation that finally broke Barnes's organization involved drug purchases as well as other classic methods of drug-law enforcement. The effort began with informants. First, the FBI arrested a flimflam man who was selling phony television sets and had a long history of such tricks. He then offered to deliver Nicky Barnes to the FBI in exchange for his freedom. It turned out that he had grown up in the South Bronx with one of Barnes's principal lieutenants and was involved with lighter drugs, like marijuana and pills. At the same time the city police in Queens found a reformed junkie who had worked as a courier for Barnes and who knew the lieutenants; he agreed to work undercover. Both informants were then turned over to the DEA, which headed the investigation.

The DEA's informants then began working their way into the confidence of Barnes's lieutenants, discovering where the organization did business, who it did business with, and how the chain of command worked. Then they began offering to do business, claiming that they knew wholesalers who needed a new source of supply and were willing to buy in bulk. These were, in fact, agents from the task force, which does the "buy and bust" operation, working from the ground up, while the DEA begins at the top.

When the undercover agents came to buy heroin, they were equipped with a microphone and tape recorder. Barnes, as usual, was nowhere in sight, but the lieutenant mentioned Barnes's name and made it clear that he knew about the sale. After the sale Barnes appeared, a fact that helped prove his involvement. Still, the police needed harder evidence, and they decided to put a tap on Barnes's phone. Barnes began doing business from the Harlem River Motor Garage, in a forbidding area of northern Harlem, and a group of federal agents went up there one freezing February night to place the tap. All the doors were securely locked, and the agents had to climb up the side of the building using collapsible ladders, crawl across the roof, which was visible from other buildings all around, and open the skylight. The agents then dropped to the floor, planted the bug, and left the same way they had come. Then they went back home to listen to some incriminating conversation. Unfortunately, the bug didn't work. They had to go back the next night, repeat the whole process, and plant another bug.

This time things went according to plan, and the agents began hearing what they had waited for. Barnes and his lieutenants used the phone to talk about upcoming shipments, make deals, and discuss how they were going to launder their cash to make it impossible to trace. Barnes revealed that he was receiving heroin from sources in Mexico and the Far East, as well as from Italians. During the time that agents were listening to these conversations, the undercover worker from the task force made his biggest buy yet—an eighth of a kilo—and once again Barnes was implicated.

By May or June of 1977 the DEA was convinced that it had enough evidence to move against Barnes. Surveillance of the Harlem River Motor Garage had proved his presence in a place used for selling heroin. The wiretap had caught conversations both by and about Barnes, connecting him to drugs. And remarks made by lieutenants to informants had proved Barnes's knowledge of what was going on. All of these sources had also provided powerful evidence against at least a dozen members of Barnes's gang. Thus, as Barnes left a favorite bar late one night, two cars blocked his path. Agents jumped out, snapped handcuffs on him, and led him quietly away. That same night, before word of Barnes's arrest spread all over Harlem, fourteen high-ranking members of his ring were quickly arrested.

The conspiracy charge was the toughest one that the police had ever tried to pin on Barnes. But this time all of Barnes's expensive legal talent and his own exhaustive reading of legal journals—he subscribed to thirty-seven of them while in jail—couldn't beat a well-knit case. He was sent to prison for life, and two of his lieutenants received thirty years each. It was the end for Mr. Untouchable. Or almost the end: it is believed that even from jail he has been controlling a considerable part of his former empire.

Part of the misery that heroin spreads wherever it goes is what it does to the police officers who are trusted to help destroy it. What happens in the United States is not completely different from what happens in Colombia or Thailand: the police are corrupted. Drug trafficking is a secret business, incredible amounts of cash are available for the asking, and nobody will be the wiser if a policeman accepts a bribe from a dealer. The police in the United States are far better paid than those in Bogotá or Bangkok, but the police everywhere feel underpaid when they consider the dangers that they face. The opportunity to cut themselves into the pie that criminals enjoy is difficult to resist, and once done, it's easily repeated.

In the 1960s and early 1970s the nation was stunned by a series of investigations into big city police corruption. The most famous of these was the Knapp Commission, which exposed the vast, almost routine corruption in the

New York Police Department. And the story told to the commission by one of its notorious witnesses, policeman Robert Leuci, became the book, and then the movie, *Prince of the City*. What Leuci revealed was that the department's elite corps, the special intelligence unit (SIU), which concentrated on spectacular drug busts, was saturated with narcotics money. By the time Leuci was finished, almost the entire SIU had been exposed—himself included.

The story told in *The Prince of the City* is that of mobsters and, above all, major drug traffickers, buying their freedom, buying information, and buying testimony from the police whose special responsibility it is to place the traffickers behind bars. Leuci recalls a routine case in which he and three other SIU members burst in on a major drug dealer and arrested him. The dealer offered $4,000 for his freedom, and the officers let him go, splitting the money four ways. But the stakes are far larger than a mere $1,000 per person. One detective boasted of having commitments of $150,000 from a South American drug dealer who was paying to have some crucial testimony changed. Another detective asked Leuci to notify a heroin wholesaler, who was a member of the mob, that incriminating information could be removed from the police file for a fee. A lawyer offered to pay Leuci for the name of a secret witness in the trial of a major violator whom he was defending; the witness, of course, would be murdered if Leuci revealed his identity. Even the "superstar" cops turned out to be deeply involved in graft. Leuci was horrified at first when Joe Nunziata, SIU's shining star, accidentally fell into one of the traps that Leuci, working for the Knapp Commission, was setting. Later it turned out, however, that Nunziata had long been on the take from narcotics dealers and was part responsible for the famous theft from police lockers of the 240 pounds of heroin used in the French connection cases. Even Leuci himself finally admitted that on at least fifteen separate occasions he had taken money from heroin or cocaine traffickers. In a situation in which graft was normal, even a good man—and most of the colleagues whom Leuci fingered he felt to be good and dedicated policemen—would give in after a while.

COCAINE

JUST AS most heroin arrives in New York, so most cocaine (as well as marijuana) crosses from Colombia into southern Florida. At one time a larger fraction of cocaine was smuggled into such other cities as New York, Houston, or Los Angeles, but traffickers came to realize the great advantage of bringing it all into the same place: they could overwhelm enforcement agents. Every year half a million Colombians pass through Miami's airport, and picking out the ones carrying cocaine is largely guesswork. If everybody who might be a mule were stopped and thoroughly searched, it would take hours for passengers to get out of the airport. Customs officials do, however, have the right to conduct a "profile" search. This means that anybody who fits the normal profile of a courier—for example, a young male Colombian—can be thoroughly searched. But unless the police have been tipped off in advance, the courier is likely to get by.

The next step is to bring the cocaine to a *caleta,* staffed by the usual array of cousins and in-laws, in Miami, or a nearby area. The real top brass of the drug organization normally lives in Colombia, but the second line of command often stays in Miami. Police estimate that 50 to 150 top traffickers live in southern Florida, along with another 200 middle-level smugglers. This concentration of so much cocaine money in one area—the marijuana trade contributes a similar amount—has made southern Florida as dangerous, if not quite as corrupt, as Bogotá or Hong Kong. Drug traffickers have turned southern Florida into yet another flashy wasteland.

Drug-related murders, often of innocent people caught in the cross fire, have made Miami resemble the Chicago of the 1930s. Miami is now the nation's most crime-ridden city; neighboring Fort Lauderdale and West Palm Beach, once a quiet retirement community, are fifth and eighth. Miami is way ahead of every other American city in the average number of murders for every 100,000 people. Somewhere between a third and half of these murders are drug-related—an amazing figure, considering how few people actually engage in the drug business. A quarter of Miami's murders in 1980 were committed with machine guns, a traditional form of gangster savagery now popular among drug rings.

Many of the murders are simply executions, committed in cold blood. Different gangs, battling for control, conduct their warfare in the streets; sometimes a gangster is murdered for holding out, as Reggie Isaacs was. Twenty-six year-old Jorge Marrera was shot in the stomach and left for dead on a street in Miami. When police arrived, he refused to talk and was taken to Mercy

Hospital. The next morning he was found in his hospital bed with a bullet through his head. The city has turned into a virtual war zone, with residents arming themselves to the teeth in self-defense. The body count finally grew so high that the county medical examiner had to rent a refrigerated hamburger van in which to store the excess corpses.

Along with the violence comes, as usual, money, and as usual the money does as much harm as good. Drugs account for somewhere between $7 and $12 billion a year in Florida, making it one of the state's three largest industries, along with real estate and tourism. And the real estate business itself has been largely fueled by drug money. Smugglers have to do something with their millions, and many of them sink their cash into opulent homes, apartments, and large real estate investments. Federal agents found eight Latin Americans connected with a drug ring who had invested $150 million in real estate. Drug money is everywhere: in the fishing industry, where the demand for boats and pilots and offloaders for marijuana is intense; in banking; and, naturally, in law enforcement, where millions go to corrupt the police. By 1990, estimates Charles Kimball, the Florida economy may be wholly dependent on drug money. What this means is that entire industries may respond to the interests of a few drug barons, rather than the needs of most Floridians. And the immense amount of cash available for expensive purchases ensures that inflation will be unstoppable.

The real key is the banking industry. Most banks struggle to get enough deposits; banks in Florida scarcely know what to do with their money. Miami's Federal Reserve bank, one of the twelve banks in the Federal Reserve System, has $5 billion in surplus currency, mostly in the $50 and $100 bills deposited by smugglers. The other eleven banks in the system put together have less available cash than that. Many smugglers simply walk up to a teller's window and shake $10,000 or more out of a bag. Not many banks will turn away that kind of customer.

Some of them, in fact, are owned by smugglers—at least four, according to drug agents. These banks can be used to make a dizzying set of transactions, which ultimately hide the original source of the money. This practice is called "laundering," and the smaller banks that do it are nicknamed Coin-o-Washes. The larger banks can actually finance drug transactions, not to mention other legitimate projects. The mysterious World Finance Corporation was opened in 1971 with $100,000. Five years later it was making international loans of $500 million. Federal agents believed that the group was financing the purchase of huge quantities of cocaine, as well as hiding the profits of smugglers. Every year, it was believed, members of the bank sent as much as 340 pounds of cocaine to Las Vegas, bringing back the proceeds in suitcases. The corporation then began to move its activities, perhaps as a result of police pressure, to a bank that it purchased and renamed the National Bank of South Florida. The bank immediately began accepting gigantic cash deposits, including $12 million in a single day, almost all in $10 and $20 bills. Authorities were unable to arrest anyone connected with the bank.

Tracing bank deposits is one of the best ways the police and federal agents have of discovering and arresting big-time smugglers. Banks are required by law to report all deposits of more than $10,000. Until recently many banks in Florida, like many banks elsewhere, didn't bother to do so; others were bribed by smugglers to keep the deposits hidden. Federal agents have tightened up on this system by creating an ongoing investigation called Operation Greenback, in which they keep track of all large deposits by means of computer. Authorities have tracked several billion dollars in drug money this way and made a number of arrests. Mostly, however, they net the smaller fish, since the larger operators have grown more careful. Many of them have shifted their assets out of the United States, at least temporarily. Often they deposit the cash in a Florida bank under a false name and then immediately transfer it to their account in South America, where it can be exchanged on the black market for the native currency.

Others create much more complex deceptions. Some of the British island territories, like the Caymans, for instance, have few of the American banking regulations, so smugglers and others often send their money there on the same planes that brought the drugs to this country in the first place. The money is sometimes deposited in the account of "paper corporations"—companies that exist only on paper—in one of these offshore banking centers, which then "lend" the money back to yet another company back in the United States. The cash is considered laundered, since it cannot be traced by government authorities like the Internal Revenue Service. The American company may use the money to make whatever investment the smugglers have in mind. Or it is always available to buy drugs if the smugglers have to sell more than they have available.

Cocaine that enters southern Florida doesn't stay there for long. The large smuggling rings are constantly dispatching couriers to stash sites across the country with fresh cocaine. The couriers will either fly or drive, depending on how large a load they have to carry. Once they arrive they go directly to one of the apartments that the group keeps to hold cocaine until a customer is ready to buy it. The apartment will be owned or rented by a low-level member of the group. Guarding a stash site is not especialy glamorous or high-paying work, and often someone who owes the gang a favor, or who has no special skills to offer, will be sent to New York or Los Angeles to sit in a safe house. Sitting, in fact, is the whole job. When cocaine is in the apartment, someone must always be there, and one of the gang's chauffeurs will bring food to this drug baby-sitter rather than let him or her leave. This guard won't touch the cocaine or sell it or talk about it or, if the police should come, claim to know about its existence. He or she is paid simply to sit, watch, and obey whatever orders come down from on high. All members of the cocaine ring have their own narrow responsibility.

Once the cocaine arrives, it is hidden. A cedar closet, if the apartment has one, is a favorite spot, since the smell masks that of the coke. The kitchen is often used for the same reason. Police who make busts frequently find baking soda or "odor eaters" scattered around the apartment; otherwise, they would smell the drug the moment they walked in.

Police examining part of the 400 pounds of cocaine, valued at more than $200 million, found on board a plane seized at Opa Locka Airport near Miami, Florida. Police jumped on the wings of the moving plane to capture the crew and the cargo. (WIDE WORLD PHOTOS)

The cocaine is almost never sold from the apartment; that might attract attention within the building. Nor do buyers come to inspect the drug or to haggle over the price. Everything is decided in advance. The syndicate's chieftains, in Miami or Colombia, know before they send out the cocaine who will buy it, how much they will buy, and how much they will pay. Predictability is a key to success. The people who guard, carry, and supervise the sale of the cocaine are carrying out simple orders that have been arranged well in advance. So are the buyers. It is, as one DEA agent puts it, "like a milk route." When the cocaine arrives, the lieutenant who has been placed in charge of it telephones the regular customer. Neither the lieutenant nor the customer mentions the word "cocaine." Like Nicky Barnes, they both know that their words may be used against them if their phone is tapped. Instead, the lieutenant says something like this: "We have some more cars in. Do you need another one like the last one?" Or they might talk about tools or tires or shirts. If they agree, the time and place for an exchange of money and drugs will be arranged.

Yet another step may come in between. Orlando Galves, a lieutenant who was entrusted with shipments of several hundred pounds, kept an office in Queens with a waiting room and a receptionist behind a desk. It stayed open from nine to five. A customer would place an order with the woman behind the desk, leave a briefcase full of money, and get a receipt. The secretary would then tell the customer when and where to show up to receive the drugs. Then she would call a courier and Galves himself. The courier would go to the stash site, pick up the appropriate amount of cocaine, and make the drop at the arranged site. Galves simply followed along in a separate car, making sure that everything went smoothly. An important wholesaler like Galves never touches cocaine and is never seen in the same place with it. His job, like that of the apartment-sitter, is very simple. He makes a few phone calls, he watches, and only if something goes wrong does he step in. He carries a weapon, but it is really someone else's job to use it.

Once the cocaine is sold, it no longer belongs to the crime syndicate. The group has made its $60,000 a kilo, and it now passes on to the second-level wholesaler. He is also, always, Colombian. From the coca leaf almost to the street, the Colombians let no one near the cocaine except their countrymen. The Sicilians have this strength in Sicily, but not in the United States. The Colombian Mafia has no weak links.

The second-level wholesalers have a smaller version of the organization of the front-line wholesaler. They have their own customers, chauffeurs, couriers, bodyguards, and apartment-sitters. They may buy as little as one and as many as ten kilos at a time—half a million dollars' worth of cocaine. Possibly they will cut the cocaine—"whack" it, as they say in the business—but more likely they will sell it intact, while doubling or tripling the price. And the customer, the third-level wholesaler, is another Colombian, who buys at most a kilo, or as little as an eighth of a kilo—about four ounces. At this level usually the cocaine will be cut, in preparation for a street sale. Only at this level does the drug leave the long chain of Colombians. The third-level wholesaler may sell directly to users or may sell to dealers who cut the cocaine further and then sell to users.

When it arrives in the United States cocaine is 80 to 90 percent pure. On the streets it is generally 20 to 40 percent pure, though it is a great deal weaker, and somewhat cheaper, when sold in the ghetto than when sold to business executives.

The Colombian network does not always work in precisely this way. A non-Colombian who has enough customers to place a multikilo order may deal with a higher level of wholesaler than usual. Mafia figures who deal in tens and hundreds of kilos make special arrangements and have their own network, which is just as elaborate as that of the Colombians. But even a major Italian dealer will not work directly with the first rung of Colombian traffickers. No one but a Colombian approaches the top of the organization. A member of organized crime who wants to deal directly with equals in Miami or Bogotá usually does so through a go-between. The Mafia knows that it cannot challenge the Colombians. The Sicilians, though it seems hard to believe, have a less efficient organization, less money, and less weaponry than the Colombians. Just as the Mafia's dominance in heroin has to be acknowledged, so does that of the Colombians in cocaine. The Mafia is completely dependent on them for its supply.

The objective of the Colombians' incredibly tight-knit organization is to ensure that nothing goes wrong. They take care of their own. Someone who is arrested can be sure that his or her family back in Colombia will not suffer. But by the same token, a Colombian who thinks about betraying the organization in any way will have to consider the power that it has over its members. It is, of course, the power to kill. In this department the Colombians are considered even more ruthless than the Mafia. Among the Mafia it is understood that families are not threatened, no matter what an individual does. The Colombians observe no such rules. Couriers or minor gangsters—who are permitted to know practically nothing about the organization, in any case—understand that if they agree to work as informants, and if they are discovered, their entire family will be murdered. The same is true if a wholesaler decides to keep some of the profits. One wholesaler fled rather than have his cheating discovered. Soon afterward his two six-year-old children were hanged, and their baby-sitter was raped and then hanged. The Colombians arm themselves like modern guerrillas. When one apartment in New York was raided the police found not only forty-four pounds of cocaine but forty-seven weapons, including machine guns and submachine guns with silencers, and several cases of ammunition. In addition, free-lance hit men are available for any assignment.

It was probably such a hit man who murdered Orlando Galves; the police rarely find out. Galves was parked in his $35,000 Mercedes at the side of a highway only a mile from his home in Queens. Probably he was waiting for a customer. According to witnesses, another car pulled alongside, and while one man stayed behind the wheel, another stepped out with both a 12-gauge shotgun and a 9-millimeter semiautomatic pistol. A few shots would have been enough to finish off Galves, but he was with his wife, his eighteen-month-old daughter, and his four-month-old son. The murderer patiently pumped at least fifteen bullets into the car, killing all four. In the car police found a handgun and $18,000 in cash. But back in

Galves's $1,000-a-month apartment they discovered 140 pounds of cocaine, worth $15 million, along with $967,000 in cash, four rifles, six handguns, and two hundred rounds of ammunition. Why Galves was murdered is unclear, though police guess that he was holding back some of the profits. Big-time operators like Galves almost never keep cash in the same apartment as drugs, since they don't want the police to find and seize both. They store the two separately so that if they're arrested they will still have, or be able to raise, the money to make bail and then flee the country. The cash that police found in Galves's apartment may have been profits that he was withholding from his superiors.

Far too few people within this network of mule and safe-house owner and front-line and second-line distributor are likely to see the inside of a prison for long. Police are, of course, interested in arresting them and seeing them behind bars, but their job is difficult, for a variety of reasons, having to do with the criminal justice system and the way that drug offenders go about their work. And this is true for marijuana and heroin smugglers and dealers, as well as cocaine.

Arresting someone presents no problem to the police. Heavily armed though most of the major violators may be, they are not Khun Sa. They cannot win a gun battle. They can, however, win a legal battle, and most of them would rather depend on their lawyers than on their weapons. In the United States, of course, a criminal must be *proved* guilty, and, when you get right down to it, it is very difficult to prove that anybody has done anything. Nicky Barnes's lawyer, for example, was once able to get him off the hook by arguing that the lease for the

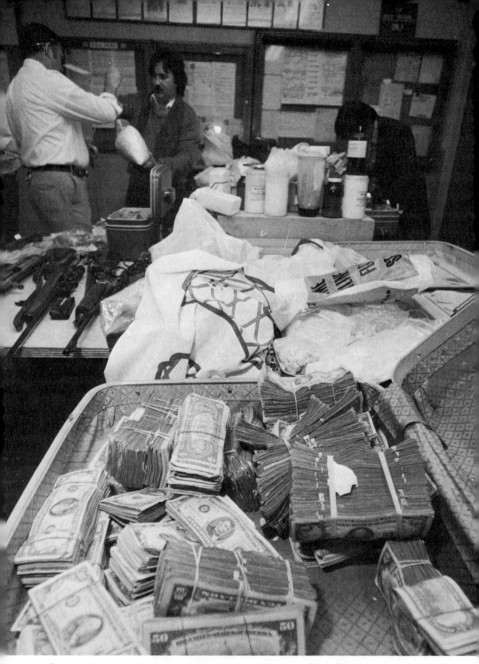

Guns, drugs, and money found in the Queens, New York, apartment of Orlando Galves, who was fatally shot along with his wife and their two young children in their car in January 1982. Police found 140 pounds of cocaine, a roomful of cash, and a number of rifles and handguns in the apartment. (WIDE WORLD PHOTOS)

apartment in which he was found along with his arsenal of handguns was not in his name.

Even more important from the lawyer's point of view are a whole series of protections to which everyone has a right in the face of police power. The police cannot enter your home to conduct a search without a search warrant. The police can't stop you outside your home and search you without a very strong likelihood that you have something illegal on your person. The police cannot search in places that cannot possibly hold what they are looking for—the so-called "elephant in a cigar box" rule. Once you are arrested, the police must inform you of your rights. They cannot pry a confession out of you. They must tell you that you have a right to a lawyer, and supply you with one if you so request. These and other rights have been established, largely since the 1960s, to make sure that rights guaranteed to everyone by the Constitution are not violated in the interest of catching crooks.

These legal protections do result in many criminals getting off the hook, because a good lawyer can often discover some error in police procedure, and the judge must then throw out the case. Many people in drug enforcement, and in law enforcement generally, feel that these rules work as a straitjacket on police efforts, and it may be that the balance has tipped slightly too far toward protecting the accused criminal. But a society that believes in the due process of law believes in it for everyone, including accused drug violators, and a society that cherishes the principle that a person is innocent until proven guilty must extend that principle to everyone.

Another problem is that many people who could be arrested are not worth arresting, and many people who could be jailed are not worth jailing. The police used to arrest street-level dealers, most of whom had been caught red-handed and who could not afford the best in legal talent. But this made no dent at all in the drug trade, since more pushers can always be found to replace old ones. The police have largely moved on to higher-level dealers, especially in marijuana and cocaine. And when the police are lucky enough to arrest a mule, who may have been caught with cocaine worth $250,000, judges often decline to send him to prison. Couriers will argue that they are innocent dupes, that somebody put cocaine in their suitcase, that they are poor peasants with hungry families back in Colombia—this part is usually true—and that they don't even understand the English language, much less the American legal system. More important in convincing judges, though, is the fact that imprisoning couriers will have no more effect on their supply than will imprisoning pushers. There are plenty more poor peasants where the couriers came from.

But people on top are even less likely to go to prison than their underlings are, and this for yet another reason that is most common with cocaine dealers: they skip bail. When major cocaine violators are arrested, the judge usually sets a very high bail, not less than $1 million. This means that the defendant must put up property equal to this amount, or cash in some fraction of this amount, in order to remain free until the trial concludes. Exactly what the purpose of bail is has never been made clear. Sometimes it is set high in response to a very serious crime, and at other times to a very rich defendant. If you escape while out on bail, the amount you have put up is forfeited; so, the idea goes, if the bail is set high enough you will not run away, even if you can post that much in the first place.

Setting bail is a bargaining process. The prosecuting attorney requests a high bail, the defendant's lawyer requests a lower one, and the judge often selects some middle ground. Major figures in Colombian families, of course, have a lot more cash available to them than most other defendants. In his testimony one Colombian defendant said that he had considered spending $20 million to buy control of Belize, a vast piece of territory controlled jointly by the British and a local government in Central America. And just as they are willing to throw away planes and boats, they will forfeit hundreds of thousands of dollars in bail.

First, though, their lawyers go to work to convince the judge that the client is not at all wealthy, is simply an innocent Colombian citizen living in a sizable house in the United States, and cannot post a large bail. Libia Cardona, as we saw, escaped this way. Jose Antonio Fernandez, the principal target of Operation Grouper, had his bail reduced from $20 million to $10 million to $500,000. Then he posted bail and quickly fled the country. Many judges simply do not realize how wealthy drug kingpins are, and they cannot believe that anyone would be willing to forfeit a bail as high as $2 million.

And all of these facts may be added to one more: courts are terribly overburdend with cases. For this reason, judges prefer a short trial to a long one. And a short trial can often be arranged if the defendant proves willing to plead guilty to a less serious charge than the one he or she was accused of. This is called plea bargaining. Defendants who agree to plea bargain may spend only a few years in jail before they come up for parole. For all these reasons combined, then, serious drug offenders do not serve much time in jail. Most are not even convicted. A 1976 study in New York's Federal Court showed that 24 percent of convicted serious drug offenders were paroled without serving any time at all; 60 percent of those who were actually sent to jail spent three years or less there; and because of parole the average prisoner served out less than half of the sentence. What this means, in effect, is that as long as you don't get killed by a rival, or your own boss, cocaine smuggling and dealing is a relatively safe business.

MARIJUANA

THE MARIJUANA business has a reputation for being much more mild-mannered than the heroin or cocaine business, yet this is only partly deserved. Many of the people who smuggle marijuana, as we saw earlier, consider themselves amateur criminals, and harmless ones, and would never connect themselves with someone like Nicky Barnes. This is even more true of the people who sell marijuana once it enters the United States. Marijuana is a lot less likely to be sold by hustlers or dope addicts than by students or people with ordinary jobs. But the closer you get to the source, the more the marijuana trade resembles the trade in other drugs. The Cubans and Colombians who control most of the business out of South America make millions of dollars from marijuana and treat it with their usual deadly seriousness. Many of the grisly murders on the streets of Miami result from the pitting of rival marijuana gangs against one another. A Cuban named Ricky Cravero who worked as a hit man for a marijuana ring boasted, after arrest, that he had murdered thirty people.

Marijuana can still be smuggled out of Mexico in small quantities of 100 or 200 pounds. This small quantity makes the complex network of front-line and second-level distributors, money-laundering and bribed bankers, safe houses and code words, much less necessary. Those who have brought marijuana across the border, or grown it themselves somewhere in the West, can get rid of it with very little difficulty. Nobody has to cut it or package it. The only necessary process is weighing out the sales, but since marijuana is sold by the ounce or the pound, rather than by the gram, a crude scale is all the equipment the dealer needs. The smuggler and the distributor are often the same person. He or she might arrive in San Francisco or Los Angeles with a few hundred pounds of marijuana in a van or camper, hold the stash in a garage, and telephone some regular customers. To each of them the smuggler would sell a few pounds, or perhaps 10 to 20, and they in turn would sell to their own contacts. And that is all that need be done to bring the marijuana to street level. It would then be sold as joints, or by the ounce. The stakes are a lot lower than in the case of cocaine or heroin, but the percentage of profit is still high. A pound that cost $200 could be broken into ounces that sell for $40 or $50 each, so that the dealer would clear as much as $500 or $600 in profit.

But most marijuana is no longer brought into the country underneath the chassis of an old car; it is brought in by the ton by highly organized groups. The same Colombians and Cubans often traffic in both cocaine and marijuana, and they use much the same methods. A group of smugglers began bringing in large loads of marijuana to Panama City, Florida, in 1977, and at first went unnoticed. Then two innocent couples happened to drive nearby while the gang was unloading a 40-ton shipment. One woman was murdered on the spot, and the other three were taken away in a truck and murdered. Their bodies were found when they washed up on shore, having been dumped into the ocean. Even in far smaller deals violence is common, since so much money is to be made. Daniel Israel Bryman was a twenty-year-old who rose high enough to act as a broker in a $60,000 marijuana deal. He went with two friends to a lonely road in the Florida keys to meet the people who were going to sell them the marijuana. But the others apparently didn't feel like selling. Bryman and his two partners were murdered.

The link between the individual who makes small deals and the kingpin who finances huge purchases of marijuana and employs a hundred or more people is that a smuggler often begins as a small dealer and ends up as a kingpin. Earlier we mentioned Donald Steinberg, a small-town boy who had a $100-million business going before the police caught up with him. One of the most famous rings in the short history of the Colombian marijuana business, the Black Tuna gang, was formed by two buddies from a working-class neighborhood in Philadelphia, Robert Elliot Platshorn and Robert Jay Meinster. The two began selling marijuana by the ounce in Philadelphia around 1974. They attracted more and more customers and began buying in larger quantities. Instead of paying someone else to bring marijuana from Florida, they moved to Miami in 1976 and made contact with Cubans who purchased directly from Colombia. Soon Meinster and Platshorn were sending hundreds of pounds up to Philadelphia from Florida.

They remained ordinary smugglers, however, until they moved a step higher and began dealing directly with Colombians. Soon they were financing boatloads of marijuana, and they were raking in cash by the million. They set up a corporation, the South Florida Auto Auction, which provided cars to transport their loads up the East Coast and to get their employees around Miami. The company also served as a source for laundered funds for use in their expanding drug business. Platshorn and Meinster became famous in the narcotics underworld of south Florida. They had a gorgeous office in Miami's famous Fontainebleau Hotel, and, though they seemed to operate a small car company, they lived like princes. The Miami Beach police watched them closely, but never found any indication of illegal activity. The two young friends from Philadelphia were in fact employing several hundred people, supplying marijuana up and down the East Coast, and Platshorn was flying back and forth to Santa Marta, in La Guajira, to arrange the purchase and shipping of tons of the weed. Still, nobody was the wiser.

Then somebody deposited too much money. A man who called himself only "H. Roberts" deposited $500,000 at the Flagship First National Bank in Miami. He had deposited the same amount two weeks before, and the DEA was already watching. The depositor's car was traced to a Miami apartment, and federal agents settled down to watch it. For two weeks nothing happened at all, and the agents were ready to concede that they had a false lead. But catching smugglers, like smuggling, consists in large part of waiting, and the DEA's patience eventually paid off. A Mercedes 450 SL finally pulled up, and a woman entered the apartment with a package. That car in turn was traced, and it turned out to have been bought from the South Florida Auto Auction, to which Meinster and Platshorn had already drawn attention by their lavish style of living.

And then something else happened. An old wreck of a trawler called the *Presidential* ran aground off the Bahamas. Nobody paid it much attention until it developed a strong smell, and the police decided to investigate. The *Presidential* turned out to have 15 tons of marijuana. The discovery of the mother ship led in turn to a bust that netted some minor smugglers and a suitcase full of receipts—a number of them from the South Florida Auto Auction.

And then the Auto Auction turned up again. It had provided bail money for defendants in the *Presidential* case. Now the police and federal agents went into high gear. They began "flipping" members of the gang to their own side to act as informants. They found out all about the Auto Auction and about the size of the Black Tuna ring. They found out that Platshorn and Meinster had planned to transfer all the marijuana from the *Presidential* to small boats and bring it into the south Florida coast. They flipped the bookkeeper and found out about the ring's finances. And they heard about the foreign mastermind, Raul Davila-Jimeno, known in Colombia as the Black Tuna. Anyone who became important in the ring received a chain with a black tuna hanging from it, so that they could identify one another. The DEA had heard more than enough, and in late 1978 federal agents moved in and arrested Platshorn and Meinster, charging them with conspiracy to sell narcotics, racketeering, and importing a controlled substance. The two boyhood friends are now serving out life sentences. The Black Tuna, however, remains at large.

The farther you get from the Colombian or Mexican end of the marijuana business, and the closer you get to the level of street selling, the more you find that ordinary people are involved. Marijuana, being so bulky, requires a great many more people to carry it around than does cocaine or heroin. Once it has been transferred from the boat or plane to some secluded place in Florida, or elsewhere in the Southeast or Southwest, it must be taken by car to its final destination. Sometimes a dealer may drive down and pick it up or may hire people to drive back and forth between the stash site and their hometown. These are the American versions of the Turkish guest workers who drive back and forth between eastern Turkey and Western Europe, unnoticed. The difference is that the Americans have no borders to cross and no checks to undergo; it is not hard work. In 1981 police arrested Geraldine and William Vandergrift, a pair of "warm, loving grandparents," as their neighbors put it, when they discovered that the couple was driving back and forth between southern Florida and Tidewater, in northern Florida, with 100-pound burlap sacks of marijuana in the trunk of their car.

When marijuana arrives in the town or city where it is to be sold, it has already left behind most of the melodrama that accompanied it along the way. Unlike cocaine or heroin, it does not have to go to a "mill" to be cut. Its owners do not have to negotiate with organized crime, because the mob takes very little interest in marijuana, a bulky and relatively unprofitable drug, especially near the selling end. Wars over turf are uncommon, since marijuana is wholesaled by thousands of unconnected people, most of whom do not have private armies of hit men, or, for that matter, guns.

Marijuana dealers have to be careful, of course, but they have much less to fear from the police than do traffickers in heroin and cocaine. When marijuana first became popular in the 1960s, police and drug agents took it as seriously as they did other drugs, and sentences for possession as well as sale were stiff. But over the years the police have concluded that they are fighting a losing battle, and in most cities the force's drug specialists will devote little time to the marijuana trade. Marijuana has become so popular in recent years that the police and federal agents would have to spend practically all their time enforcing laws against it to make much of a dent in the business. And few people feel that marijuana trade. Marijuana has become so popular in recent years that the police and federal agents would have to spend practically all their time enforcing laws against it to make much of a the business. And few people feel that marijuana poses the kind of threat to society that stronger drugs—not only cocaine and heroin but pills and chemicals like PCP—do.

So large is the overall drug problem that the police have to choose their targets carefully. In many places even the cocaine business, not to mention marijuana, has to be passed up in order for the police to concentrate on heroin. At the federal level the DEA still mounts major investigations into the workings of the big Columbian and American smuggling groups. But once marijuana disperses from Florida or Texas or Georgia, in small loads, to every state in the nation, there is little that enforcement authorities can do to prevent it from being smoked. As DEA agent Abraham Azzam says, "There's not much we can do to cut off the flow of marijuana or even cocaine, so long as they're socially acceptable."

IV
WHAT IS TO BE DONE?

IN THE world of narcotics-law enforcement, nothing seems to work completely forever, while some things fail totally and swiftly. Narcotics agents often feel outflanked, outnumbered, and sometimes even outgunned. Their enemies have 100 or so times as much money to spend as the authorities do. What's more, the police, unlike criminals, have to use legal methods: they can't murder, bribe, or terrorize people who get in the way. It is frustrating work, and the frustrations come quickly to the surface in conversations with narcotics agents. They

144

are frustrated with district attorneys, with judges, with politicians, with a "permissive" public. The public, in turn, often takes a dim view of the activities of narcotics agents. Many people think of "narcs" as burly types who knock down doors to arrest a college student for smoking a joint. But neither the police nor the DEA, as we have explained, spend much of their time arresting people who smoke or sell small amounts of marijuana, though they have in the past. And few people would object to the goal of wiping heroin off the face of the earth, which is the primary concern of most federal, state, and local drug-law enforcement agents. Those who fear the destructive influence of both the business of drugs and the drugs themselves have to agree that narcotics agents perform a vital service. Yet drug-law enforcement has probably never received the commitment it ought to have.

Yet would all the commitment in the world wipe out drugs? Probably not, not as long as people are willing to pay for them, and places are able to grow them. The problem of drug-law enforcement is incredibly complicated. In this book we have dealt with three different drugs—heroin, cocaine, marijuana—at three different points—within the borders of the drug-producing country; from that nation's border to the United States; and inside this country. Different enforcement techniques are used for each drug and at each point. They have all contributed something to decreasing the flow of drugs, but all in all the best that can be said is that they have prevented a tidal wave. The disasters that are predicted— Southwest Asian heroin flooding the United States—like the successes that are predicted—so much marijuana seized that the supply will dry up—never seem to appear. The price and purity and quantity of drugs rise and fall, and wind up where they were before.

The greatest difference between stopping the flow of narcotics and stopping bank robberies or embezzlement is that the largest part of narcotics crime occurs beyond the reach of American law. The farmers who grow the crops that become narcotics are Colombian or Bolivian or Pakistani or Burmese; American anti-drug laws cannot touch them. The gangs who buy the drugs and smuggle them are South American or Sicilian or Chinese; we can only work with those in their home country to stop them. And both the farmer and the smuggler are often beyond the power of the government under which they live. The Sicilian gangster or the Pathan peasant are laws unto themselves. What can we do, far away, to control their activities?

Without the help of the Colombian or Pakistani or Thai government, we can do nothing. With them, though, we can reach into the lives of peasants far enough for them to feel that cooperation is a healthier choice than defiance. Most farmers grow cocaine or opium because it brings in more money than do other crops. The government has little to offer as an alternative. Here a great opportunity is being missed. Peasants don't become rich growing these crops; they don't expand. In order really to change their lives they need many things that only a government can offer them: low-interest loans, cheap fertilizer, new sources of income, roads into town, education for their children. Smugglers cannot bring development; only direction and aid from the government can do that. And the more dependent people become on the government, the more dangerous and foolish the growing of crops for smugglers begins to seem. And the more presence the government has in a village, the easier it is to enforce laws against the growing of poppies or coca or marijuana. Drugs are grown in areas where people are very poor or where the government has little authority. The government could gain greater control by helping peasants out of their poverty. Rural development, with help from both the United States and other industrial nations, is going on throughout poor parts of the globe, those that grow drugs as well as those that don't. But such programs remain few and far between.

And the United States can do nothing unless the host government is committed to helping the poor. In many of the crucial countries—Bolivia, Pakistan, Burma—this commitment is hard to find. Mexico was able to wipe out much of its drug-growing problem in part because it was eager to provide lawful alternatives to its peasants. (Mexico was also lucky—it discovered oil in the early 1970s.) And the government must, of course, be committed to the touchy problem of crop destruction. The left-leaning government of Peru, for example, has taken rural development seriously, but many of its crop destruction efforts seem to have been performed for the benefit of photographers. There is much anxiety among those familiar with the international drug situation that illegal opium may emerge from Turkey once again, since the Turks felt that they were pressured by the United States into outlawing and policing the destruction of the crop in the first place. Some of the Turkish political parties remain tied to poppy farmers.

The United States has no influence at all over some of

the key countries in the drug trade, though today's enemy may be tomorrow's ally. Iran is undergoing a revolution, Afghanistan a civil war; Laos is closed to practically everyone; Bulgaria is firmly in the communist bloc. But with those countries with whom we have good or even decent relations we must work to prevent the creation of new Golden Triangles or NWFPs or Bekaas—areas under the control of rebels who do not acknowledge the government. This probably means trying to satisfy these rebel clans and tribes as often as it does trying to crush them. Their demands for more liberty must be taken seriously, in exchange for more cooperation with the government. Efforts by the Pakistanis or Burmese to destroy all threats to the power of the central government have only angered the tribal people. The United States has a role in persuading these countries that helping the poor, and granting more liberty or self-rule to local groups, is in their own interest. And we have a role in helping to pay the high costs of development.

Once drugs leave the country where they were grown, they disperse in so many directions that they are practically impossible to keep up with. The complex network that drug criminals have developed must be matched by an equally complex enforcement network. Police officials from different countries must work together and share information. The DEA, for example, had a long-standing relationship with Italian police, but allowed it to lapse after the smashing of the French connection. Only now, after Golden Crescent heroin has been pouring through southern Europe, has the DEA realized that the Italian *carabinieri* are their most important contact.

In the cat-and-mouse game of drug smuggling, the law

of the weakest link often applies. Drug smugglers will look for the one place where enforcement standards are weakest, and they will send their supplies through there. Southeast Asian traffickers used to send all their European heroin to Amsterdam because the drug laws in Holland were so weak, though this is no longer true. Now they avoid Japan, because of the thoroughness of its customs officials and the sternness of its courts; instead they use traditional smuggling capitals like Hong Kong. The burden of drug-law enforcement is a constant effort to close loopholes. Just as each new country where fields of opium or coca or marijuana spring up must be organized to fight them, so each new smugglers' haven, whether Hong Kong or the Bahamas, must be shut off as soon as it opens.

Smugglers, too, have their weak links. Heroin from the Pakistan-Afghanistan border must be taken overland on the long route to Italy, at least until someone else takes the place of the Sicilians and Corsicans. The smugglers must use highways; they must cross borders. From Turkey they must cross through Bulgaria to take the northern route. Bulgaria is the only country through which they must pass that does not seem to take the border check seriously. If the Bulgarians would check vehicles as seriously as do the Yugoslavs, the drug river could be narrowed, perhaps a great deal. The same is true for Greece, to the south.

The weak link in the case of marijuana is La Guajira peninsula. The area has been run by smugglers for generations, and their unquestioned control has made it possible to bring thousands of tons of marijuana there to be loaded into ships and planes. The Colombian government has made a serious effort to reclaim this area, staking out the tiny airstrips carved into the jungle, interrupting shipping from the coast. This may have had some effect, since smugglers have apparently been moving inland to avoid the police. Taking the coastline away from smugglers is probably even more important than destroying marijuana, since thousands of tons have been torn up or burned with no noticeable effect. Without La Guajira and nearby areas, however, mother ships could operate only to the West Coast, unless they tried to pass through the Panama Canal. La Guajira, however, is a long way from police control, as is much of Colombia.

Once narcotics enter the country, the DEA, along with state and local forces, can go to work. But the problem is almost too large to handle: too many Colombians are climbing off planes in Miami with cocaine strapped to their chest; too many thousands of miles of jagged coastline are accessible to speedboats and mother ships. But the real business of narcotics-law enforcement is not to go after drugs, but to go after smugglers. The big drug rings can lose practically any quantity of narcotics, not to mention low-ranking members, without being hurt. The DEA zeroes in on its list of major violators—the men and women who actually run the business. But the battle between big traffickers and enforcement agents has been, at best, a standoff. Few are so careless as actually to handle drugs. And without this "smoking gun" the police often cannot build a strong enough case against them, though they know the smuggler's identity and even the size of his business. Only recently have narcotics agents begun to learn how to use conspiracy laws. Another tactic is to prove that the trafficker has received huge profits that he has not reported on his tax form. Famous mobsters like Al Capone were finally jailed on charges of tax evasion, and federal officials are now mounting similar investigations against smugglers. Colombian cocaine trafficker Jaime Araujo was found guilty in Los Angeles of failing to pay taxes on $13 million of income—the biggest tax evasion case ever. Methods like this are essential in order to combat organized crime, especially with the revival of the Sicilian connection, but the DEA, the FBI, and the Internal Revenue Service have not proved very successful in applying them so far.

But all of these efforts to decrease the supply of drugs may come to nothing if the demand for drugs is not also diminished. Perhaps nothing can be done about marijuana and cocaine, which are so widely accepted. Yet tales by professional athletes and entertainers whose careers have been ruined by cocaine habits may change the belief that cocaine is harmless; obviously, it is not. And the continuing campaign to prevent heavy marijuana use, especially by teenagers, may also make people hesitate.

But neither of these problems, of course, compares with that of heroin addiction. Addicts will pay practically anything for their fix, so great is their desperation. And the desperation of addicts equals the profits of smugglers. As a congressional committee report in 1980 stated, "Such staggering profits make international trafficking worth almost any risk and render it practically invulnerable to law enforcement." Research into ways of curing, or at least controlling, heroin addiction, as the committee pointed out, is essential. Methadone clinics, which provide an addictive but much milder drug, need continued funding, at least until something better is discovered.

But we must also understand that the addict joins hands with the peasant in Southeast Asia or the Golden Crescent to form a grim circle of poverty and despair. People inject heroin, as they grow opium, because they see no alternative. Addicts, like peasants, must feel that there is another way out. From their position of dependency they cannot help themselves. Help must come from the outside. We in the United States may grow indignant over the failure of countries like Burma or Turkey to provide a better life for their people. But until we show our own willingness to provide a better life for the slum-dweller who may become an addict, to conquer his despair, our words are meaningless.

BIBLIOGRAPHY

Daley, Robert. *Prince of the City*. Boston: Houghton Mifflin, 1978.

Del Corso, Det. Stephen, Det. Bill Erwein and Michael Fooner. *Blue Diamond*. New York; G. P. Putnam's Sons, Inc. 1978.

Kamstra, Jerry. *Weed: Adventures of a Dope Smuggler*. New York: Harper and Row, 1978.

McCoy, Alfred. *The Politics of Heroin*. New York: Harper and Row, 1972.

Messick, Hank. *Of Grass and Snow*. Englewood Cliffs, N.J.: Prentice-Hall, 1979.

Robertson, Frank. *Triangle of Death: The Inside Story of The Triads—The Chinese Mafia*. London: Routledge and Kegan Paul, 1977.

Sabbag, Robert. *Snowblind: A Brief Career in the Cocaine Trade*. Indianapolis, Ind.: Bobbs-Merrill, 1976.

Staff and Editors of *Newsday*. *The Heroin Trail*. New York: New American Library, 1974.

INDEX

About
the
Author

JAMES TRAUB is a graduate of Harvard University. He has traveled and taught in India and also written articles from there for *Saturday Review* and *Politics Today*. He has been associate editor of *MBA* magazine and a senior editor of *Saturday Review*. He now works as a freelance writer and is the author of *India: The Challenge of Change*.